... pray ...
book to be
to you
inspires you deeper
with Christ! May God
and encourage you through
book. In Jesus' name.
amen!

—La Genia Sims, 2020

Grace
over
Perfection

Mercy, Grace, and Love
are the Standards

Choosing a Lifestyle of Jesus

ISBN: 978-0-578-70215-5

All scriptures are taken from The Holy Bible, King James Version and New International Version, New King James Version, and New Living Translation.

Book cover design and interior formatting
by Luminous Publishing. LuminousPublishing.org

Printed in the United States of America.

First printing edition 2020.

Table of Contents

Introduction

As I was considering why this topic of Grace over perfection is so important, one pivotal factor caught my attention: *believers looking to themselves.* Allow me to explain further. Today, some believers measure their position in Christ based on their actions. They are allowing their efforts to determine their salvation, their preservation (or sustainment) in God, and their justification in Him. I often witness individuals—Holy Spirit-filled, born of the water and the Spirit individuals, depending on themselves for their salvation and preservation in the Lord. Depending on their self-perceived measure of perfection to keep them in their walk with Christ—*as if man could save and sustain himself, in his strength.*

Do you find yourself trying to clean up the mess of sin in your life by your mere strength, trying to rationalize and pardon the effects of falling short of God's revealed standards? Or do you even answer the door when the weight of condemnation comes knocking at your front door? Or better yet, do you hold yourself (and thus others) to a standard of perfection that *you* think it takes to be saved? And then when you fail (because we will never reach perfection in a world of brokenness), you beat yourself up and become your own

1

worst critic? Is Grace even a thought for you when you fall short of God's glory?

Please don't misinterpret me. I know exactly how this feels because *I've been through it.* Subconsciously, I wanted to be severely perfect and "right" in my relationship with Jesus that I couldn't fathom the reality of falling short in His sight ***in the slightest way.*** I did not want to fall short before Him even if it meant that I failed at reaching an added goal or rule to our relationship that He didn't give me to add in the first place. *I know how it feels.* Past experiences, hurts, and pains enabled me to be judgmental of myself--not allowing the Grace of God to rescue me from the weight of falling short. I know what it feels like to want the approval of Jesus severe enough to beat yourself up when you fall short of His revealed standard. Believing that you're not good enough for Him and His love every time you fall short of His standard, *which this isn't the truth but is a device Satan uses to keep the children of God from experiencing true freedom in Christ.* To become a present-day Pharisee of others, when you *do* find yourself getting it right because, "Hey, I earned it. Right? Everyone should commit to what I commit to doing in my relationship with Jesus because I'm doing it perfectly." Hey, I'm being vulnerable here and may be exaggerating a bit for the sake of giving you a picture of the bondage of perfection that I entangled myself in for so long. The kicker is, without me even realizing it! *Trust me, I understand.* If you identify with these same struggles, allow me to share something with you.

In 1 Corinthians 15:9-10 NIV, the apostle Paul is speaking of how he is the least of the apostles because he persecuted the church before his conversion, and he makes a profound, foundational statement for the Christ-follower today that is worth paying attention to. He says, "But by the grace of God I am what I am, **and his grace to me was not without effect**. No, I worked harder than all of them—yet not I, but the grace of God that was with me." He's essentially saying I am who I am today because of the Lord's Grace in my life, but then he says, it was not gifted to me in vain or without effect because I put it into effect, I worked it, and I worked it hard. Paul understood something that could change the life of the believer today, that Jesus pours out His Grace upon us, and it is poured without vain when and *if we dare to operate in it and not against it.* Working against it would be not allowing it to take effect in our lives but rather rejecting it because we can't get past ourselves. When dealing with Grace, we have to get past ourselves to receive it.

If you look around, you'd see that's not the posture of every Christian today. **We** want to be the one to save ourselves; we want to be the one to keep ourselves through our actions; we want to be the ones who forgives ourselves, rather than to allow Grace to take effect in our lives. Imagine if Paul would have never received the Lord's Grace throughout his lifetime. Imagine if he would have beat himself up for his past and not put into effect the Grace that was given to him by the Lord Jesus. Paul would have never made it to where he did in the Lord without the impact of Grace in his life. Notice Paul says He worked harder than the rest of the apostles because of the Grace of God over his life. Not his grit, not his ability to do the right thing or follow a specific set of rules, but it was the Grace of God that brought him to where and who he was. Paul worked God's Grace; he understood that there are blessings in the covering of God's Grace; he realized that there *is* favor in the Grace of God.

That's so different from the mindset of most believers today. Why is it so hard for us to be at peace in working the Grace of God in our lives? What is it about the concept of Grace that makes it so hard for us to receive it freely? Why would we rather condemn ourselves, and in our shame, cover ourselves and play a game of hide-and-seek with the Lord rather than allowing our shortcomings to propel us to the feet of Jesus--to the throne of Grace? You see, my Friend, God knew we'd need a sacrifice and knew we couldn't save and keep ourselves. That's the beauty of the Gospel of the Lord Jesus; *He covers where we fall short and allows His Grace to aid in keeping us.*

It was in my gravest sin that Grace met me. Growing up without my dad and feeling the weight of neglect, abandonment, and rejection caused me to fill that void with drinking, sexual behavior with men, drugs, and other dysfunctional behaviors. The fulfillment was never permanent but always temporary (rather I realized it then or not). It was Jesus--clothed in Grace that saved me from the weight of sin in my life (Ephesians 2:8-10 KJV). It was not me coming to my senses or trying to fix myself before Him. It was **HIM** coming as the Ultimate Superhero to save me and to allow for

His Grace to be what covered the sin I knew by nature. You see, I knew sin all too well—but God saved me and has kept me from it. Not because of my actions but because of His Grace. *Don't get me wrong, though.* Yes, I had to submit to the Lord. A submission that said, "Lord, I haven't done it right all this time and **can't** walk in your righteousness by myself because **it's You** that makes me right. Not what I do or how perfect I perform—it's only by your Grace."

The enemy, Satan, can sometimes use our desire to be right with God against us in a way that keeps us from walking in the freedom that comes with the Grace of God. *Not the freedom to fulfill the desires of our flesh and the lusts thereof (Romans 13:14 KJV) but the freedom to allow Grace to propel us further in our walk with Christ (as it did for Paul).* To let Jesus shield us from the fiery darts of our righteous acts being what fulfills God's law and standard because truth-revealed, they don't have the power **(in and of themselves)** to do so. The Bible says our righteousness is as filthy rags (Isaiah 64:6 NKJV) and, therefore, cannot keep us, but only Jesus, our Heavenly Father, can do that.

Satan could also use our desire to be right with God to his advantage when our participation with sin exposes our nakedness in the presence of a Holy God. Let me explain further. When we sin, we can get caught up in taking what we believe are necessary actions to cover ourselves from the shame, embarrassment, and condemnation of sin. We can begin attempting to shield ourselves from the effects of sin, and by default, end up hiding from the Grace of God. For

Adam and Eve in the book of Genesis, it was covering themselves with the leaves from the fig tree. For you, it could be drowning yourself in the tears of shame and guilt. It could be that you choose to punish yourself by utilizing righteous acts or spiritual disciplines [**without** the intent to put your flesh under subjection]. Either way, our desire to please God can be used against us if we are not careful and if we are not operating in Grace. Grace forgives; Grace gifts mercy without condition; Grace pardons—and it's only the Grace of Jesus that can save us, protect us, cover us, cover the weight of our sin and propel us forward in Him. Operating in the Lord's Grace is an area we all could use assistance in. Will you choose to walk in Grace or in spiritual guilt that never really propels you forward, but rather, keeps you bound to the weight of condemnation and sin, which Jesus didn't create you to carry anyway? That's why He died, child of God. Rest in Him.

My prayer is that by the end of this book, the Lord would compel you to submit your heart and actions to Him, knowing you can't save yourself and realize that you need Him to be the One who pardons your sin because you, by yourself, cannot. I pray that you'd recognize the Grace of God to be what saves and keeps you; that you'd allow the Grace of God to be what detaches the *weight* of your sinful nature from you and acknowledge Him, my Friend, to be what makes you white as snow and not your righteous actions because they simply cannot.

It is the righteousness **from Him** that causes us to behave righteously, not vice versa. Our righteous acts are not what achieves righteousness. Righteous deeds cannot save us, but the One who makes us righteous or "good" saves and keeps us; the One who justifies us is who saves and keeps us; He's Who makes us--*well, right*. My prayer is that by the time you finish reading this book, you'd know this.

For your context while reading, during part one of *Grace over Perfection* (GOP), I will be revealing what Grace is, the **truth** of Grace, and the **deceit** of perfection. During the second part of GOP, I will be sharing what Biblical principles are needed to pursue Jesus and a lifestyle of GOP. (Note that they're listed in their order intentionally; therefore, without living out the preceding one, you cannot effectively live out the latter). Now that we have laid our groundwork. Let's dive in!

Part I

Let's talk Grace and Perfection!

CHAPTER 1

❧

What is Grace? No, really.
What is Grace?

"Christ is become of no effect unto you, whosoever of you are justified by the law; ye are fallen from grace."
~Galatians 5:4 KJV

In December of 2018, I served at my organization's missions conference called Urbana in St. Louis. It's a students' mission conference we hold every three years to encourage, inspire, and compel students to God's purposes in the world. During the third day, I realized Jesus was doing something--*different*. Initially, I couldn't make sense of it, but then something broke—it began to make sense. I went to the prayer room. The feeling of healing and restoration that I would soon discover the Lord to be doing in my life had changed the course of my life. As the process of a caterpillar to a butterfly, my life wasn't what it was no more.

During the first couple of days of the conference, the Lord gently brought to my attention that I can be prone, or more naturally inclined, to judge others (especially Christians) based on my perceived expectations of what they do or don't do "to remain saved." I would witness someone's actions as a Christian and determine in my mind the kind of Christian they were and subconsciously think (depending on their actions), "They aren't a real Christian—they aren't 'living it' *for real, for real.* What are they doing? They couldn't possibly have been transformed by God—they haven't entirely given their lives to You, Jesus." God had something for me to learn during this trip.

You see, it never really was about their actions and what their efforts proved about them. It was about my heart and why I felt the need to judge, hold, and label others to my perceived standard of what a Christian exemplified. Holding them to rituals that, in reality, was birthed from my insecurities and what actions I felt **I needed** to do to be "right" or in *sound, right* relationship with God. You see, the situation was so much bigger than I thought. *I will not get into why this is a problem too much right now, but we will dig into it later in this book.*

So, the Lord revealed to me my judgmental ways towards others, their walks with Him/their faith in Him, and how I do the same to myself, even. The thoughts were no longer "ok" for me to have; they didn't feel right or even fair; *how could I be judgmental towards God's creation, the same demographic group the Lord was calling me to influence?* The Lord was beginning to give me an uneasiness about these things.

While coming to the realization of these things, a coworker and I decided to go to the prayer room; *we were initially going to stay for an hour.* Yeah, right, who was I kidding? As I walked into the studio to receive prayer ministry, I was hopeful but also fearful. I was excited for God to reveal to me what He was doing inside of me. However, I was too afraid of the ugliness of my heart that the Lord could also uncloud amid Him revealing His will. As I received prayer and prayed with one of the prayer ministers, Jesus confirmed to me that the way I was judgmental to others, *I was doing it to myself as well.* The judgmental **standards** of perfection/a perfect Christian that I was putting on myself, I was also putting on others, and vice versa.

Allow me to give you the backstory. You see, when I was about four years old, my dad left my life to pursue other work endeavors, and during the time he had left, my dad and I were extremely close, *with me being heavily attached to him.* Therefore, my dad's absence caused me to validate my worth and value in others' acceptance of me *and not Jesus.* To explain more clearly: when my dad left, Satan used deception to falsely communicate to me that my dad left because I simply wasn't good enough for him to remain present in my life. *Essentially,* my dad's absence birthed insecurity in me that allowed me to search for my worth and value in others' assessment of who I was (i.e., my personality, physical appearance, etc.). This insecurity allowed for the void of neglect to plead with the hole in my inner man--*my soul cried out for acceptance and inclusion.*

What I found out that day in December of 2018 was that I judged others because of the pain and neglect of my past with my earthly father, which had caused me to be quick to judge myself. In my relationship with Jesus, I had adopted the mindset of thinking I had to do things perfectly before Him or else He'd leave me. The danger of this for me was that I cherished what we had so much so that I couldn't fathom Him abandoning me--I had wanted to be "right" before Him all the more. Although I knew (so I thought) that Jesus wouldn't leave, I did think there was something I couldn't do "right" that would cause Him to leave me. I'd mostly believed there was something I **had** to do to keep my relationship and position with Him. I mean, I had to spend time with Him every morning before starting my day, right? It's written in the Christian code that we inevitably have to pray elegantly, right? I mean, we have to be perfect to remain in Him. *Right?* **Absolutely** not. The dysfunctional fruit from my past experiences as a four-year-old little girl had begun to make room for me to judge myself to a standard of perfection with the Lord, which in return made room for me to judge others to that same standard.

The thought of my actions caused me to mourn—it disturbed me, and it caused deep-rooted repentance in me. It was at that moment that Jesus declared His love and acceptance of me in a way that I had never felt by Him before. That day Jesus let me know that **He** was here, pursuing a relationship with me because **He** chose to be, not because of anything I could ever do or not do but because **He**

wanted to. That, my Friend, is Grace, and it changed the course of my life that day.

Grace is a Choice

Biblically, Grace can be known as, by definition, "God's free and unmerited favor for a sinful humanity." A good Pastor friend of mine even stated once that, "Grace is illogical." Grace is illogical mainly because *Grace is a choice*. It says, "Yes, I could leave and abandon you, but I'm not," "I could cut you off right now…your actions seem deserving of it, but I am not going to." Isn't this the exact opposite of what society teaches us? I mean, we're taught that if they "cross" you, cut them off--only forgive them when they have repented from their actions. Seriously, the human mind cannot grasp the concept of Grace because next to our sinful nature, society, and media teach us to operate in opposition to the Grace that God gives us. This **very** concept is why it is illogical.

So when we begin to try to understand the Grace of God, we are distracted by how a perfect God could offer us mercy and Grace for everything we've ever committed **against** Him. We're confronted with thoughts similar to, *"How could a Holy God operate in Grace when dealing with a sinful humanity?"* We find the answer in God operating in a fashion that is opposite to what media, society, and even our families teach us. Isaiah 55:8 NLT explains it best, "'My thoughts are nothing like your thoughts,' says the Lord, 'And my ways are far beyond anything you could imagine.'" Rather than to cut us off, the Lord desires to forgive; He desires mercy over judgment. Though He is a just God, He'd much rather us repent from our wicked ways that His Grace may excel into effect in our lives.

In Matthew, chapter 9 (starting at verse 9), Jesus is having dinner, fellowshipping with tax collectors and 'sinners' at Matthew, the tax collectors' home when the Pharisees ask the disciples about why Jesus is eating with such a group of people (the tax collectors and 'sinners'). Jesus responds in verse 12 that it is not the healthy who need a doctor, but the sick. However, the verse I want us to focus on is verse 13 when Jesus says, "'But go and learn what this means: I desire mercy, not sacrifice. For I have not come to call the righteous, but sinners.'" Jesus is saying something revelatory and transformative here; He is essentially saying that He has not come to call the righteous, but those who hold the awareness to their need of Him. The righteous, in this case, being those who gratify themselves by the standard of themselves—born again believers who seek and aim to save and keep *themselves* according to their righteous deeds (i.e., their rituals, sacrificial worship practices, etc.), *especially those without surrendered hearts and complete devotion to the Lord.* Our righteousness is of filthy rags—God does not want our righteous **acts**, by themselves alone. But what God desires is faith in, dependence on, and a devotion to Him that **produces righteous deeds**.

Jesus has **not** come to call the righteous but the sinner. The one who operates out of **mercy**; the one who knows they are a sinner, *by nature*; the one whose heart is devoted to God and yet, knows they need and seek after Grace. The one who knows their need and seeks after mercy. You see, mercy deals with our heart's posture, our knowing we can't save ourselves; it deals with our devotion being to God, and God does not desire our rituals without our complete commitment to Him. An outward expression of faith cannot hold and keep us alone. It is our inward faith that drives and motivates our works and outward appearances of faith to and *for* the Lord. The Life Application Study Bible describes this concept by stating, "God doesn't want sacrifices; he wants our loving loyalty." He does not want our works, without our complete devotion to Him; He wants our dedication first and our good works to flow from that devotion. That on the day we need mercy from Him, we'd understand our righteous acts, *alone*, cannot obtain it for us, but only devotion to Him can do that; *only relationship can do that.*

To expound further, Lamentations 3:22, 23 NLT reminds us that, "The faithful love of the Lord never ends! His mercies never cease. Great is His faithfulness; His mercies begin afresh each morning." God, out of His faithful love towards us, desires to have mercy and compassion on us. He wants for His mercies--forgiveness, out of His loving-kindness and faithful, steadfast love, to keep us and not our righteous deeds, *even if they are **for** Him*. How much would our lives change if we *truly* understood this? That every time we fall short of God's revealed standard, every time we sin against Him, that the Grace of God is waiting for us—waiting to save us, waiting to help us--to have mercy on us. He is waiting. He isn't waiting to condemn us, but rather, He's waiting to keep us, restore us, and sustain us. Our relationship with Jesus supplies **so** much more than condemnation for the frailties of our human nature, but rather, Jesus invites us into Grace and not religious deeds or works with the fear of not doing the right thing. *Living our lives in spiritual bondage (that which is driven by works and not Grace) because we've submitted to traditions, rituals, deeds, practices, etc. that are not rooted in Grace or devotion to the Lord but are yet rooted in works that we hide under the umbrella of holiness.*

An Orphan Child vs. A Son

Consider, with me, how our lives would truly be transformed by us coming into the *full* knowledge that Jesus desires for Himself (out of His mercy, goodness, compassion, and loving-kindness) to be the One who keeps us. He does not will for the counterfeit version of *ourselves* (in the form of our righteous deeds) to do so. I believe that our ability to understand that Jesus wants to be the One who preserves us can be discovered in if we carry the countenance of **an orphan child** or that of **a son**. An orphan child describes a born again believer who's bound to the yoke of slavery in their relationship with Jesus--even after being freed by God, Himself, through Jesus. A son describes the believer who **understands** that they are adopted *by* God and **free** from the yoke of slavery. *Notice that both are free; however, one (the orphan child) isn't aware of their freedom.* **Therefore**, they consistently find themselves bowing or giving in to the bond of slavery. At this point in reading, you may be thinking,

"What, LaGerrica--what're you talking about?" Stick with me--allow me to explain further.

Galatians 4:21-31 NKJV says, " **21** Tell me, you who desire to be under the law, do you not hear the law? **22** For it is written that Abraham had **two sons**: the one by a bondwoman, the other by a freewoman. **23** But he *who was* of the bondwoman was **born according to the flesh**, and he of the freewoman **through promise**, **24 which things are symbolic**. For these are the **two covenants**: the one from Mount Sinai **which gives birth to bondage**, which is Hagar— **25** for this Hagar is Mount Sinai in Arabia, and corresponds to Jerusalem which now is, and is in **bondage** with her children— **26** but the Jerusalem above is **free**, which is the mother of us all. **27** For it is written:

'Rejoice, O barren,

You who do not bear!

Break forth and shout,

You who are not in labor!

For the desolate has many more children

Than she who has a husband.'

28 Now **we**, brethren, as Isaac *was,* **are children of promise**. **29** But, as he who was born according to the flesh then persecuted him *who was born* according to the Spirit, even so *it is* now. **30** Nevertheless what does the Scripture say? 'Cast

17

out the bondwoman and her son, for the son of the bondwoman shall not be heir with the son of the freewoman.' **31 *So then, brethren, we are not children of the bondwoman but of the free.*"**

In Genesis 16, Sarai (before she was Sarah) had borne Abram (before he was Abraham), no children. So she decided that she'd have her husband Abram go into her servant girl, Hagar; Sarai's goal was to obtain children through Hagar. It worked--Hagar bore Ishmael. Now, because Ishmael came from the maid (Hagar) and was born according to the flesh, Hagar's descendants would be in bondage. However, we (as God's born again, adopted sons and daughters) by inheritance are of the free woman. Therefore, we must not walk [as though we are born according to the flesh] in the ways of one who is bound to the law--not walking in true, spiritual freedom in Christ Jesus.

The spirit of the bondservant (Hagar) is one of an orphan--one without a home. The spirit of the freewoman (Sarah) points to one of true sonship. *One of true freedom in Christ.* When we possess the heart of an orphan, according to Trish and Jack Frost [founders of Shiloh Place Ministries], we (for example), see God as our Master (*which is true*), while neglecting Him as a loving Father. We serve because we want to earn God's favor; rather than serving from a place of pleasure and delight in Jesus. Another example of the countenance of an orphan could be sensing God's presence in a way that's conditional and distant rather than close and intimate. Romans 8:15 NKJV says, "For you did not receive the spirit of bondage again to fear, but you received the Spirit of adoption by whom we cry out, 'Abba, Father.'" This scripture is what true sonship is. Having the luxury of crying out, "Abba, Father!" Not only inheriting this luxury but utilizing it, as well, notably when missing the mark. The Greek word for adoption in this verse literally means "the placing as a son (i.e., adoption), and Christian sonship in respect to God." God sacrificially made it so that we would have sonship in **HIM!** John 14:18 NKJV embodies this saying, "I will not leave you orphans; I will come to you." The Lord does not will for us to be as the bondservants child, but to fully walk in our inheritance as the freewoman's child.

When we walk in the spirit of bondage again to fear (Romans 8:15 NKJV), we fear not doing the right thing. We fear the fleshly, imperfect nature of our being. We fear what us missing the mark "proves" about our identity and the security of our salvation. We fear the shame and guilt that comes with not getting it right. When we submit to a works-based Christianity (meaning we base our relationship with Jesus off of performance, traditions, rituals, deeds, etc.) in our relationship with the Lord, we are burdening ourselves, again, with the yoke of slavery. *We are walking backward in the spirit of bondage to fear when Christ has instead given us the Spirit of Sonship.* This concept will continue to unravel as you advance in your reading of this book; you will **precisely** understand what I've explained about the countenance of an orphan child and a son of God by the end of this book.

CHAPTER 2

ॐ

What Perfection Says

"That's why I take pleasure in my weaknesses, and in the insults, hardships, persecutions, and troubles that I suffer for Christ. For when I am weak, then I am strong." ~2 Corinthians 12:10 NLT

Y'all, can we have a moment of transparency? Around the first week of January 2019, I noticed that growing within me was thoughts of jealousy, envy, and comparison. These fleshly feelings would arise at random times, never with random people but oddly enough, with those who were closest to me. When I had first started experiencing these thoughts, one of the things that bothered me the most was that I couldn't control them. *They would come whenever they wanted.* At whatever hour, second, and minute that they wanted, and even though they were unwanted thoughts, they kept rising, and **I** simply couldn't control it. I mean, *I had zero control.* There was no prayer that I prayed to make the thoughts go away, no crying, no shouting that made them go away in their entirety. *You get the point.*

Anyway, I found myself trying to fix them, and because **I** couldn't fix them, **I** thought that there was something wholly impaired and dysfunctional about me. *I felt that the presence of those thoughts was telling me something about myself.* More specifically, I thought that the presence of those thoughts was telling me that I *was* those thoughts. I rationalized that the thoughts of jealousy, envy, and comparison were proving to me that I was, in fact, jealous, envious, and a comparer of others. This deception is *precisely* what the enemy wanted, and you know, so many of us, as I did, fall into this trap today. Believing that the sinful actions, thoughts, feelings, etc. we are being tempted with are, in return, telling us **who we are**. *Boy is this so far from the truth.*

Instead of looking within, or internally, we allow what's manifesting outwardly via our actions to communicate to us what's taking place on the inside [and though often this can be the case, at other times it isn't]. The danger in this is that we could begin to try to solve an issue with a solution that is rooted in a totally different cause. For example, we try to refrain from anger that leads to temper tantrums when the source is deepened sadness and depression that came from growing up in a broken home where your father may have physically abused your mother every Friday after a long day of work. If you're not careful, you'll spend your time attempting to refrain yourself from temper tantrums when the **internal or more profound rooted issue** is that you need healing in your heart from the trauma you experienced as a child.

Further, what we do is: instead of looking *internally to discover* what's the root cause of our sinful actions, *we see how the root is being manifested, outwardly, and begin to lose "it!"* Instead, we need to consider what the enemy is using to cause sinful behavior and discover the rooted-issue. All of a sudden, one thought is determining our entire identity. It sounds so silly, but honestly, we all fall into this trap so often in our everyday lives. How does the enemy deceive us with this tactic, you wonder? Simple. My theory is that we've gotten so used to allowing outward actions to be the sole thing that determines and mirrors our devotion to Jesus. The problem with this is when we see the negative side (our sinful nature, the brokenness of humanity, the parts of our soul that haven't yet been made whole or healthy, etc.) to this mindset manifesting, we begin to think that our identity lies in the sinful action, nature, or the brokenness of our humanity. **Not so**. Our sinful nature does not determine our identity in God. However, the conflict you'll find in this works-based salvation is that the more you see your brokenness (or your humanity) manifesting, the more you'll think you're not getting it right (or the more inadequate you'll see yourself). Also, if you're basing your devotion to Jesus on your actions-the more you find yourself falling short of perfection, the more of a hole you'll believe you're in.

When we began to see the negative sides of this works-based salvation, we began to adopt a mindset similar to thoughts that contain words like, "Clearly my actions, solely, determine my spiritual condition and state? I mean, to walk with Jesus, my fleshly nature will not rise, right? Because I'm walking in the spirit, I should never see a manifestation of the flesh, right? I should never see my brokenness, right?" I believe that when it comes to experiencing recurring thoughts, temptations, and attacks that we ought to seek the Lord about where the **root** of those thoughts, temptations, and attacks are coming from and not solely the thoughts, temptations, and attacks themselves.

Simply put, we need to get to the root cause of the fleshly thoughts, temptations, and attacks. What's feeding your fleshly thoughts and temptations? Your fruit (actions) could be revealing a root issue, internally because our actions are not always revealing what genuinely is. *Only the root of the problem could do that.*

Let me explain even further by sharing more of my journey with walking through dealing with thoughts of jealousy, envy, and comparison. I kind of shared the story a little earlier, *actually in chapter one*. However, after being so attached to my father as a little four-year-old girl, and then him leaving my life (what seemed) so abruptly, I'd innocently allowed **his departure** to leave me believing I wasn't good or worthy enough. More specifically, I had innocently allowed for his departure **(alongside the schemes of the enemy)** to determine my worth, my value, and my dignity. I believed that I wasn't adequate because he left me. *I mean surely if I were, he would have stayed, right?* No, this mindset was so far from the actual truth.

And so from that point on, I began to live my life feeling like I had to prove myself to others and prove *why I **deserved*** to be in their lives. I believe this is where the root of perfection was born because I was always consumed with doing the right thing *to* remain in the right standing with others—to keep my place in their lives. My life had become an "**If** I do the right thing, **then** they'll stay" kind of scenario. "**If** I make myself to be who I'm noticing they like their friends being, **then** they'll want to be around me;" "**if** I could be the kind of girl he likes or show him why I'm the girl he *should* like, **then** he'd like me;" "**if** I am the perfect girl for him, **then** he'd choose me." I had begun to allow my relationships and friendships with others to become an **if, then** kind of relationship. In fact, this was a mindset that breathed over into my relationship with the Lord.

You see, I was so used to (based on what I had seen in the past from my earthly father) believing that if I did this, then Jesus would do that. More specifically to my situation, I adopted the mindset of if I continue to do these things, then I'd remain in right relationship with Him. *Which is **such** a trick of the enemy, but it was what I was familiar with from childhood.* What I had seen was that I had given my all to my earthly father, and he left, and upon him leaving, I soon associated his absence with the lack of who I was. So, therefore, it was nothing for me to think that I had to do things perfectly, or a certain way, for Jesus to be satisfied in His decision to choose a relationship with me and keep me justified in Him. And you know what? The problem wasn't that I needed to stop allowing myself to produce "if, then" effects. I needed to allow the Lord to minister to me concerning who He had created me to be and the identity I have in Him; that I am adequate. I am enough in **HIM** and that He chose me because **He** decided to and **not** because of who I was, who I am, or who I would become. This example is what I mean by dealing with the **root** cause and not with how the root is manifesting itself outwardly. Oh, how much do we miss the mark if we don't understand this essential truth? *We love Him because **He first** loved us (1 John 4:19 KJV).*

When discussing our struggles with perfection together, a sister in Christ, stated that perfection is rooted in approval. Isn't that so true? We become obsessed with doing everything right to a "T" that if we feel like we aren't doing *what determines perfection for us at that moment* then we are not right or justified with God. What drew me to perfection was the feeling of neglect that produced the insecurity of inadequacy, so what the enemy used to attack me with jealousy, envy, and comparison was the root of inadequacy and neglect that came from my father leaving me. Isn't that funny how that works?

The very thing that we are actually struggling with can be shielded or rather distracted by the physical manifestations of the works of the flesh that originally was given space to "shine" because of that place or area of struggle in our lives (and like I said for me, it was neglect and inadequacy). It's not even the real, underlying issue, but we began to focus on that one thing. Think about when you go to a concert, and they have an artist who is opening up for the artist whose concert it actually is; the opening artist only had room to shine because of the artist whose concert it *actually* is. *You see? The only reason why the temptation, that's **presented** to you, seems so desirable is because of the struggle **within** you that has not yet been restored by your Creator.*

The truth is that when we don't know the truth that God speaks over our lives—and any past experiences—we can fall victim to the lie that the enemy tries to speak over our lives **and** past experiences *through* temptation. We're prone to doing this because we believe that the temptation that is pleasing before us (because of the area of struggle within us) is the actual problem when in reality, it's the opposite. The struggle area within us (i.e., inadequacy, neglect, etc.) is what needs to be addressed rather than allowing the enemy to use the temptation to be something that determines who we are, or how "saved" we are. The danger in allowing your temptation to define you is that when you see the temptation presented to you, you can begin to think you **are** the temptation, that you **are** the problem, rather than the sinful **action that is in the temptation**. *(Oh, how do I wish we'd understand the depth of this).* To add, the danger in this is that if you find yourself *falling* into the temptation (aka saying yes to the temptation), *you can also begin to think that you are the problem, rather than the sin living **in** you.*

In Romans 7, Paul is describing his tension between wanting to do the right thing but instead, doing that which he hates. In verse 15, he states, "I do not understand what I do. For what I want to do I do not do, but what I hate I do." Verse 16 goes on to say, "And if I do what I do not want to do, I agree that the law is good." In verse 17, Paul states something that is a gamechanger; he says, "As it is, it is no longer I myself who do it, but it is **sin living in me**." There it is right there for everyone to see. Out in public with no garment to cover it. *Sin lives in us*. Even as baptized, Holy-Spirit filled name bearers; *sin lives within us*. If we are not careful, when walking in the ways of the Spirit (intentionally trying to follow the Spirit of God), if we don't understand that sin lives in us, we can begin to allow for perfection to tear us apart. We will start to look at our actions, and how right we do things—all the time—to be something that determines our place and our salvation with the Lord. We can begin to see our works as our salvation tool—we can begin to see our relationship with the Lord to be something we do and not something that is gifted to us by the One and true God. Something that just--*is. Not something we have to work for and not something that we have to walk in perfection to keep.* Yes, we do have our part, but our role isn't to get it right every single time, our part is to surrender in complete devotion to Him that our works may flow from that place, by the Grace of God. Because here is the thing about getting it right every single time, the moment we don't get it right, we began to question our entire salvation. We began to question our place with the Lord; we began to allow something (sin) that doesn't have the power to do so to determine our salvation. What's of the flesh doesn't have a right to decide nor determine anything of the Spirit. So, if you are of the Spirit—if the Spirit is your new nature, sin no longer has a right to determine anything about you!

Now, we also can't find ourselves on the other end of the spectrum and blame everything on sin, either. As I said before, the only reason we agree to the fleshly temptations and thoughts is that something deep within us--some issue(s) deep within identifies and agrees with the sinful temptation(s) and/or thought(s). Some thing(s) within the depths of our soul needs some intense healing.

A Word on the Soul of Mankind

Our souls are made up of our mind, will, and emotions. Our mind is the area of our soul that knows, considers, and remembers. Psalm 139:14 NKJV says, "I will praise You, for I am fearfully *and* wonderfully made; marvelous are Your works, and *that* my soul **knows** very well." Lamentations 3:20 NKJV says, "My soul still **remembers** and sinks within me." Knowing and remembering are both functions of the mind. Our will is the area of the soul where we make decisions, choose, refuse, and seek. Job 7:15 NKJV says, "So that my soul **chooses** strangling *and* death rather than my body," and Job 6:7 NKJV says, "My soul **refuses** to touch them; they *are* as loathsome food to me." Choosing and refusing are both ways that "the will" functions. Lastly, our emotions are what express love, hatred, joy, grief, desire, or any other kind of feeling. 1 Samuel 30:6 NKJV says, "Now David was **greatly**

distressed, for the people spoke of stoning him, because the soul of all the people was **grieved**, every man for his sons and his daughters. But David strengthened himself in the Lord his God," and Song of Song 1:7 NKJV says, "Tell me, O **you whom I love**, where you feed *your flock, w*here you make *it* rest at noon. For why should I be as one who veils herself by the flocks of your companions?" To be bitter and love are both emotions, and they stem from our soul; *our emotions, will, and mind points to what is in our soul.* The problem is that our experiences can paint a mural in our soul. What's in our soul is not genetic; what we experience, the different battles we walk through, trials, tribulations all take part in what's in our souls. And if we experience traumatic experiences that leave its footprints on our souls—we eventually begin to release what's in our soul. This reasoning is why soul healing is essential; from the inside out. If we don't heal, we will almost always desire to produce tainted actions, *or at least, it'll be a struggle not to do so.* God wants to heal our souls to experience true freedom in Him.

So back to what I was writing before, the moment we don't get it right we began to think things like, "Oh, I need to do this, something isn't right with me," "I need to put into place some sort of spiritual discipline because I'm tripping." And, *of course*, there's no problem with spiritual disciplines, but what I want to share is the problem with putting it into place in response to not getting it right. We can find ourselves beginning to take action based on the manifestation of a sinful action **(dealing with the outside)** without doing the work of uncovering where the sinful **action** flowed from *(the* *root cause of everything).* To give you a better look at this and yes, it's a bit graphic *(I warned you).* If you had been vomiting for the past few days, it would be crazy for you to see you vomiting to be the sole issue without first looking at why you are vomiting. What did you last eat? What kind of experience did you have in the past, in the form of what you last consumed to cause you to vomit today? Did you go to a new restaurant? Did they seem like a clean and reputable restaurant to eat at? *Does this create a better picture?* If you are constantly falling into sin, having sinful thoughts--the falling into sin isn't the main problem; it's **a** problem, but not **the main problem**.

What I want us to be able to look at is: what is the reason **why** I am falling into sin? What is it about that particular sin that's so appealing to me? What is it about the act of having sex that is causing me to have sex outside of marriage? What is it about cursing at everyone that offends me that every chance I get to do it, I do it? What is it about making others feel less than that makes me feel better about myself every time I do it? You see, it's not just because of your sinful nature; we can't take the easy way out and just blame it on our fleshly nature. Take it a step deeper. *Why is it easier for you to fall into this particular sin and not the other kinds of sin?* It was easier for me to fall victim to the thoughts of jealousy, envy, and comparison because there was something more deeply rooted in me. The neglect and inadequacy that was deeply planted within me, I had not yet known the truth of what the Lord spoke over my struggle with inadequacy, neglect, and insecurity.

Can we be real, Y'all? Jealousy was easier for me to fall into at that time because I hadn't yet allowed the Lord to speak the truth of who I am in Him while experiencing those feelings and thoughts of inadequacy. I hadn't yet done the work of allowing Him to show me that His presence in other people's lives wasn't His neglect to me. That's what Satan does in jealousy, envy, and comparison; he highlights others' lives so much that we temporarily forget the significance and uniqueness of our own lives. That's his trick! If we are not confident and secure in who we are in the Lord, we *can* be easily moved by Satan's attacks concerning the works of the flesh. **Someone needs to hear this.** This portion of the book was not in my plan to write about because this isn't what this book is about, necessarily, but I'm going to go with it anyhow. I had to first learn for myself that every thought that I have *isn't from me.* Satan has the ability not to read our thoughts but give us thoughts. And after weeks…months of walking this out with the Lord, I had learned what Satan was doing. If you could imagine with me, what Satan would do is take something that was on the outside of me (jealousy, for example) and would present me with it. I would be so consumed with why I was having the thoughts and with what I thought was wrong with me for having the thoughts that I neglected to take to the Lord what Satan was using to present me with jealousy, *which was the inadequacy and neglect.*

So by the time I'd considered why the thoughts were present *and what was wrong with me for having these thoughts,* **I had gone in an entire circle.** By the completion of the circle, I would have been accepting the jealousy, saying, "yes" to it because I wasn't secure enough in my adequacy in Jesus. You see? What started as a temptation that was presented to me, I began to claim as my very own, as something that was a part of me. I'd begun to treat thoughts of jealousy, envy, and comparison as intentions that came from within me when instead, the feelings were merely presented **to** me. The two are different, you know? [And we have to be careful not to fall down the rabbit hole of accepting the Devil's schemes]. *However, my insecurity, along with the improper understanding of how the enemy uses vices like jealousy, made room for me to accept it.*

If you are struggling with jealousy, envy, and comparison today, Jesus wants you to know that you are enough in Him and that someone else's gain isn't your lack. He has given you special gifts--special and unique ways to bear His name; special and unique ways to exude and show Him off well, **that's only specific to you**. *There's something special and unique about you that no one else on planet earth possesses.* If you can imagine us sitting down near a peaceful ocean, having a heart-to-heart, as I speak these words of Life to you, allow for the Holy Spirit to help you through these tormenting thoughts. *I want you to become confident in the way that God has uniquely, fearfully, and wonderfully formed and made you.* Don't beat down on yourself to the point you don't take this to the Lord and seek Him while walking through this. Allow Him to reveal to you what it is about you that no one else can possess or what it is about you that allows you to represent Him in ways that no one else can. Do this so that when Satan tempts you with discontent-filled thoughts like jealousy, envy, and comparison, you'll respond in a way that shows you're sure and confident in the uniqueness of who you are and the uniqueness of **your** portion and not that you are uncertain of those things. Be encouraged by who you are in Jesus, not saying yes to Satan's temptation that gets your eyes off of the beauty of your portion because you're witnessing the beauty of someone else's portion. Both can co-exist together. That's the beauty of our Jesus—He creates us all in special ways that altogether glorifies Him perfectly. Allow for the Lord to show you how to glorify Him best ***with your portion***. He makes no mistakes; you are who you are in Him today because of His beautiful portion to you, the unique portion that He trusted you to steward. *Steward it well, my Friend.*

Not Allowing Perfection to Rule over *YOU*

We say no to perfection by seeking Jesus despite our flaws and imperfections. There becomes a point in your walk when you realize and come face-to-face with your frailties as a human; you won't get it right every *single* time, but the more important area of concern is: what do you do when you don't get it right? Do you become downcast in spirit, taking a bath in the condemning sorrow of your tears? Do you automatically put on your superman cape and strive to save yourself out of your mess, picking up the pieces that Christ already picked up when He submitted His life on the cross for you? Or do you fall at the throne of Grace [as He is waiting for you with open arms], pursuing (saying yes to or choosing) repentance not with your strength but with His? In 2 Corinthians 12:6-7 NLT, Paul is telling his readers how He

33

was given a thorn in the flesh to keep him from boasting and being exalted above measure for the abundance of revelation that he receives. He says, more specifically:

"If I wanted to boast, I would be no fool in doing so, because I would be telling the truth. But I won't do it, because I don't want anyone to give me credit beyond what they can see in my life or hear in my message, even though I have received such wonderful revelations from God. So to keep me from becoming proud, I was given a thorn in my flesh, a messenger from Satan to torment me and keep me from becoming proud."

Paul then notes that he asked the Lord to take it away three different times (which most likely means Paul asked on three different occasions) and each time the Lord responded, "My grace is sufficient for you, for My strength is made perfect in weakness" (12:9 NKJV). The Lord's response is why Paul declares that he will glory in his infirmities, reproaches, necessities, persecutions, and distresses for Christ's sake because it is then that Christ's power rests upon him—it is when he is weak that he strong (12:9,10 KJV). Beloved—Friend, we must take on the same mindset. When we see the weaknesses of our flesh, our first move need **not** be to handle things in our own hands, fixing them in our strength. But rather, when we see the weakness of our flesh, we must first realize and know that when we are weak, we're truthfully, then strong in Him because of His power that rests on us. Thus we're better off falling at His feet, making room for the Holy Spirit to sanctify us in our imperfections, rather than [like Adam and Eve after they had fallen in Genesis 3], taking things in our own hands. We take things in our own hands by doing things like covering ourselves (Genesis 3:7), hiding from the Lord (Genesis 3:8), and other actions of the like that prove we don't see God as our true Father, *who we can run to and never away from. He wants to save us in our weakness by resting His power upon us when we are too weak, even for ourselves.*

CHAPTER 3

୫

What Grace Says

"Therefore, since we have been justified by faith, we have peace with God through our Lord Jesus Christ, through whom we have gained access by faith into this grace in which we now stand." ~Romans 5:1-2 NIV

When I'd first started experiencing thoughts of jealousy, envy, and comparison, I would feel these emotions rising and would begin to freak out because, "Lord, how could *I* have these kinds of thoughts? Where are they coming from? *How can I fix myself out of this one?*" Seriously. *I was so perplexed as to how **and** why I was experiencing these thoughts in the first place; however,* the danger was that while I was experiencing these works of the flesh, I began to associate them with my identity, and allowed them to be a determiner of how valuable I am. I would think thoughts close to, *"Clearly, there's something wrong with me. **I'm defective and am a horrible person. Right?**"* Not so.

When I first noticed these thoughts becoming a frequent situation, everything within me wanted them to go away, and I would cry out to God about why and how they were too much for me to handle and about how I didn't want them to be present. I would frequently remind Him of the toil these thoughts were having on me and causing me to exude. *I mean, talking about an attack from the enemy? I felt like I was continuously being thrown into the fire.* But I thank God for this process now because you see, it was through walking in this process that God gave me understanding about a concept that is so crucial to the Christian walk; ***while the Spirit within us is at work, so is the flesh.***

The Flesh vs. the Spirit

The point in which Jesus saved us, there became two natures at war with one another, within our members—*the flesh and the Spirit.* In Ephesians 2 NLT (verses 1-2 specifically), the Apostle Paul is talking about how, when before we were born again, we followed Satan and the ways of this world as the children of disobedience do today. However, in verse 3, he notes something very important. *It's almost like when you're in conversation with a friend who is telling you a story, and they quickly brush over a part of the story that's extremely important, but then they brush over it like it's not.* If you don't pay attention closely enough, you could miss **the fullness** of verse 3. *Let's review it together!* Ephesians 2:3 NLT says, "All of us used to live that way, following the passionate desires and inclinations of our sinful nature. By our **very**

nature we were subject to God's anger, just like everyone else."

Paul is saying here that within us is the **very nature**, *even while we are saved*, to be enmity (which means to be hostile) against God. He is essentially saying that given our natural inclinations, *as sinful humanity*, we were subject to God's anger, just like everyone else. What this reveals to you and me is the reality that our flesh, our sinful desires, our sinful nature is constantly waging war against our very own soul (1 Peter 2:11). There's good news, though! When we are saved (born of the water and of the Spirit according to John 3:5,8 KJV), deposited into us is the Gift of the Holy Spirit. It is at that point that we are then empowered to walk in the ways of the Spirit, and it is when we walk in the Spirit that we will not fulfill the lusts, *or natural inclinations*, of the flesh—which is so ever-present within us.

Author Pete Scazzero, in his book titled, "The Emotionally Healthy Leader," describes what can be identified as a form of the works of the flesh as *the shadow*. According to Pete, "Your shadow is the accumulation of untamed emotions, less-than-pure motives and thoughts that, while largely unconscious, strongly influence and shape your behaviors...the shadow is *not* simply another word for sin." Pete also notes that the shadow, or the fleshly nature, can reveal itself in sinful behaviors such as judgmental perfectionism, outbursts of anger, jealousy, resentment, lust, greed, or even bitterness. The shadow can also reveal itself through subtler, unnoticeable actions like:

- A need to be liked by people and rescue others

- A need to be noticed

- An inability to stop working

- A tendency toward isolation or harshness

What does all of this mean, LaGerrica, you wonder? Well, if within you is a natural inclination to be enmity to God and you're allowing the Holy Spirit to help you walk in the ways of the Spirit, you can be assured that there is Grace for you. You have to understand that Jesus is the embodiment of Grace---*He **is** Grace!* We hear this all the time, but I question if we truly allow it to sink in: Jesus died for our sins---past, present, and future. He knew that we couldn't and would not ever be able to save ourselves. This truth is why it is foolish to look to *our* actions, *our* rituals, *our* works to save ourselves. Seriously. Think about this for a second. Jesus willingly submitted His life for our transgressions because of our propensity to sin. Only a Perfect Savior could redeem and position an imperfect people in right standing with the Father. He died because He knew what we *would not* be able to do—*follow Him in perfection*, according to His standards and ways of living.

It is once we are saved as a born-again believer, however, that Jesus calls and declares us righteous. It is not because of us and our actions but because of Him and what **HE** did and because we acknowledged and received His finished work. We did not gain the term righteous because we earned it but rather because we inherited what He already was and is--*righteous*. The Apostle Paul, in Philippians 3, declares that he desires to be found in Christ, not having a righteousness of his own that comes from the law but rather **the** righteousness that comes **from God** and is **by faith**. He is essentially saying that he wants his righteousness and faith to be found in Jesus and not in himself. *You know?*

There are a few "different kinds" of righteousness that are described and portrayed in the Bible. One being a righteousness that's merit-based (*meaning I do, He gives*). Another being a righteousness that's by the law or acting in a morally correct manner (this is the righteousness of the law Paul was speaking of in Philippians 3), and the other being a righteousness that's in Jesus—being correct by the **declaration** from Him. God's heart and desire are for us to be found abiding in **the righteousness** that's in and from Him because **He** declared it to be so and not because **we** earned it--*or because we feel like we did, anyway.* Paul understood something we all can afford to understand today: our righteousness, our justification, our worth, and our value are found in Jesus and what He did and not in our perfect works, *or even the imperfect deeds. Let this revelation free you today.*

To take it a step further, in the Gospel of Matthew, Jesus is recorded explaining to John's disciples that His coming was not to do away with the law, the old religious system of Judaism with its rules and traditions. But rather, as one who wouldn't patch old clothing with new clothing or one who wouldn't put new wine with old wineskins, His goal in coming down to earth was to add something "new" to the Judaism law system/structure. Jesus' goal was to offer forgiveness of sins and reconciliation to God—the epitome of the Gospel. He offered forgiveness, Grace, and mercy; *He offered Himself.* Jesus wants us to turn from sin and to Him--*even in the presence of our sinful nature.*

Think about Ephesians 2:8-9 NIV, "For it is by grace that you have been saved, through faith—and this is not from yourselves, it is the gift of God—not by works so that no one can boast." And honestly, the truth is, *and I can most definitely relate,* sometimes we can find ourselves doubting and questioning how genuine our salvation is because of and in the presence of our flesh acting up (showing itself to be present). We find ourselves feeling inadequate or unworthy because of the effects of the sinful nature. I get it, but the truth *also* is, God desires for us to understand that He came to save us from the effects or consequences of our sinful nature—which is death. And so God, in His righteousness, holiness, and perfection, makes it so that through the power of His Spirit that fills us, we can be sanctified, which is why I continue to stress this important factor that we cannot try to fix the defects of the sinful nature. We cannot fix ourselves, but it takes a Holy God--in our submission to Him--to sanctify us and make us right, *not based on our actions but based on our turning to and surrendering to Him in our sinful condition.*

You know what else? Jesus desires our righteous deeds to come from our devotion to Him. Not the other way around.

He doesn't want us to produce righteous deeds in attempts to get or be right with or even closer to Him. Jesus doesn't care about our righteous deeds in the same way that He cares about our **devotion** to Him. Great! You do things a certain way and have certain routines that you practice (and don't get me wrong, *some of these things may **actually** be healthy to the Christian life*) and you produce particular works to keep you in "perfect" (*which is a form of comfortability, honestly*) relationship with Him; the truth is that it is not those works that will keep you in Him, but it is in your heart's posture and your devotion to Him that you will be kept; your heart must be pure, cleaned out (Psalm 51:10), and in the right condition before Him. So, it is pivotal that we understand, as sons and daughters of the King, that our devotion to Him is what Jesus uses to preserve us in Him and what produces righteous deeds-through the sanctification process. It is not the opposite. *Our righteous deeds **do not** showcase evidence of the sanctification process.* That is **not** how it works. *Because then you open yourself to the possibility of dealing with your works not being genuine but instead being a behavior modification that doesn't produce long-lasting fruit.*

Choosing Grace

God works **through our imperfections,** and so you wonder what Grace says—what *Jesus* says? Grace says, "It doesn't have to be perfect for God to work through it." Simply. Put. As. That. And so, with me dealing with the increasing number of sinful thoughts at the beginning of 2019, I had to learn and realize that there was a nature within me that was enmity to God. This *nature* was aiming to produce the works of the flesh (being jealous and envious, along with other works of the flesh). I had to realize that there was nothing wrong with me—*I'd just come face to face with the works of the flesh.*

You better believe this was difficult for me because I'm inclined to "make sense" out of **every** detail in my life (*I know*), *preferably without imperfection;* **what** a fitting picture of the brokenness and dysfunction that came from the neglect and abandonment I'd experienced as a little girl. As I mentioned earlier, I didn't understand where the thoughts of jealousy, envy, and comparison were coming from. I *surely* didn't like them, and if I'm honest with you, they produced feelings of shame within me. Therefore, in the midst of me not feeling in control and feeling all kinds of uncomfortableness within me, I naturally wanted to make sense of it all. I've learned; however, it's much more freeing to take my flaws and surrender them to Christ, trusting Him to deal with and make sense of everything (or **not** make sense of everything; whatever He chooses because **He's** the One that's God). *Mostly, I've learned to allow for Him to handle and take care of my flaws and me.* Trusting that He knows the discomfort I'm experiencing (Hebrews 4:15 NKJV) and will see me through because of His understanding.

You see, where before I was more inclined to take things into my own hands when I didn't feel in control of what was happening in me, I 'd began to learn that sanctification wasn't found in me handling things on my own hands but was found in my surrender to the Spirit of God at work within me. **Thank God for this!** Because what essentially began to happen is me deciding to allow this situation to help me to have more trust in the Lord and **not *my*** abilities. [My prayer is that you'd truly understand this]. I truly learned what it meant to surrender to the Lord, having the faith and trust in Him to believe that in His perfect timing, He would work His perfect will (that which is initiated by Him and not me) **in** me.

Here is what I learned during this time of travailing in finding **the core** of my identity amid imperfection:

- Because you notice the **works** of the flesh manifesting **within** you **doesn't mean those works of the flesh are a part of you.** When saved, there is a **strong** difference between your identity (what Jesus says) and what threatens that (the works of the flesh).

- Life **is not** a cookie-cutter. If we were to bake cookies together, a cookie-cutter would help us to shape our cookies exactly the way we desire to. Now, if we utilize the tool correctly, our cookies would turn out to be shaped perfectly. However, in our lives, this does not always turn out to be the case. We don't have a cookie-cutter that helps us to shape, plan, and mold our lives in the exact way we desire to. Life throws us curve balls at times, and sometimes we will see our fleshly nature in ways that we don't desire too. In life there will be times when we don't feel in control enough to be able to shape and carve out the details of life in the way we most desire to; but even then, God has the power to work through the ragged ends of our cookie that is in our flesh. However, the good news is that we can learn to accept the imperfections of life while we trust the Lord, with dependence on Him, to sort through them. It won't always look—*Well, pretty.*

- Along with the last point, walking in Grace makes it one step easier to accept the imperfections of life; this is more freeing for the follower of God because you can liberally trust the Lord while He works out the kinks in you, preparing you for eternity with Him.

- By focusing on the Grace of God and not on our imperfections, we are putting God on the throne and dethroning ourselves.

- You do not have to fix what you think you need to fix about yourself to feel **enough** in your relationship with God. **He**, himself, makes us enough and justifies us and anything He wants to work out in us, He will do as we yield to His Spirit in our day-to-day life; and not as we put together a plan (for example and though not in and of itself bad) to sanctify ourselves.

- Every thought that surfaces in your mind do not have to be rationalized in *your* strength. The reason is that even though it comes from a good place/a pure heart you're focusing too much on yourself and not on **Jesus.** 2 Corinthians 10:4-5 NKJV says:

"For the weapons of our warfare *are* not carnal but mighty in God for pulling down strongholds, casting down arguments and every high thing that exalts itself against the knowledge of God, bringing every thought into captivity to the obedience of Christ,"

Make it a priority to learn how to bring every thought into captivity to the obedience of Christ that doesn't line up to obedience in Him and after you do that, *practice trusting the Lord and not worrying about anything further.*

This example is how we choose Grace. We choose to allow the Holy Spirit to sanctify us in our flesh, our pitfalls, our wounds...*our shadow.* You know, there are times when you'll find yourself walking after the Spirit, as Romans 8:1 KJV covertly instructs us, "There is therefore now no condemnation to them which are in Christ Jesus, **who walk not after the flesh, but after the Spirit,**" and you will *still* see and feel your wounds and the works of the flesh. For me, my wounds arose from feeling neglected and inadequate as a four-year-old child. For you, it may be wounds that birthed from rape, molestation, or even wounds from not receiving enough attention from a parent in the household while growing up. *Hey, I get it.* And you know who else gets it, as well? Your Heavenly Father.

It was through experiencing an increasing number of thoughts of jealousy, envy, and comparison that I discovered that Jesus was doing an important work in my inner-man. He was pruning me to cause me to bear more fruit in Him (John 15:2 NKJV), speaking to my heart what His Grace was saying, and letting me know that I was still His--no matter what I was experiencing. Grace, being Jesus, was speaking to me that different seasons have different times, according to Ecclesiastes 3, and this was my season to learn that his Grace is sufficient even in the midst of me feeling like I was falling apart. This season was my opportunity to learn more of who He is and how powerful His Grace is, even when I feel my weakest; to allow me to see how gentle, patient, and kind He was toward me when I was too weak and judgmental to even be those things to myself.

Because here is the thing (if you're anything like me), when seeing these wounds alive, real, fresh, and ever-present within you, your inclination would be to drawback and not engage with yourself *or even with others*, in the ways you did before. But it is in the midst of that very tension of knowing **and** believing what God says about you [while the presence of the works of the flesh is most strong] that you **NEED** to engage with the Holy Spirit like never before because it is in **that very place** where Grace abounds even more. For clarity purposes, the works of the flesh I'm speaking of here are found in Galatians 5:19-21 NKJV. The Apostle Paul informs us:

> "Now the works of the flesh are evident, which are: adultery, fornication, uncleanness, lewdness, idolatry, sorcery, hatred, contentions, jealousies, outbursts of wrath, selfish ambitions, dissensions, heresies, envy, murders, drunkenness, revelries, and the like; of which I tell you beforehand, just as I also told *you* in

time past, that those who practice such things will not inherit the kingdom of God."

When we commit to walking after the Spirit, we will not walk after the things of the flesh. *Don't get me wrong.* The works of the flesh will form (meaning they will tempt you), but as long as we are walking after the Spirit, they will not [and cannot] prosper (remember Isaiah 40:31 and Isaiah 54:17 NKJV), unless we allow them to. The presence or **rising** of a particular work of the flesh does not mean, Son and Daughter of God, *that it has prospered. It only prospers if [and only if] you choose to give in to it.* Otherwise, don't get discouraged when you see the sinful nature rising, but as a lion going after a zebra--**EAT!** That sounds pretty aggressive, huh? Yeah, I know.

Nevertheless, you must know that just as a lion would become aggressive in the presence of its lunch, we should become aggressive in seeking after God's own heart, intent, and truth in the presence of our sinful nature—*especially when we are being intentional about walking after the Spirit, and not the flesh.* In John 6:56 AMP, Jesus reveals, "He who eats my flesh and drinks my blood [believes in Me, accepts Me as Savior] remains in Me, and I [in the same way remain] in him." When pursuing the Holy Spirit and your flesh rises, get your heart in alignment with Him. Eat of His flesh, drink of His blood [**and I'm talking** *spiritually*] that He may remain in you and you, in Him while He's pruning, healing, taking away and making healthy what needs to be pruned and cleaned out of your heart, soul, and mind for *His* glory.

Part II

*Life with Jesus and Walking
in Grace over Perfection*

CHAPTER 4

&

Accepting His Love for You

"In this is love, not that we loved God, but that He loved us and sent His Son *to be* the propitiation for our sins." ~I John 4:10 NKJV

It was July of 2019, and I found myself in a counseling session; I actually remember this day clearly because I was excited and anticipatory while waiting for the outcome of my first meeting. As we went on with the intake process, the therapist responded to why I told her I was seeking counseling by saying, "Ok, I see. You want help with accepting others and being forgiving." I was immediately taken aback…" *What do you mean I'm seeking help in accepting others and in being forgiving?* I didn't say that…" I brushed her words off with hesitancy as we finished with our initial meeting, but then (in the months to come), her words would begin to stick with me, and I would ponder on them from time to time. *"You want help with accepting others and being forgiving."*

Acceptance

Acceptance can be defined as "**the action of consenting to receive or undertake something** offered." The part of the definition that I want to focus on is *the action of consenting to receive or undertake something.* Now I would perceive that the something offered that is spoken of here could be something preferred--*or not preferred*; even still, one **chooses** to consent to receive or to undertake it, rather it is preferred or not. *This explanation is a perfect picture of what the Lord did for us.*

Romans 5:8 NKJV says, "But God demonstrated His own love towards us, in that while we were still sinners, Christ died for us." Even while we were sinners, before we were saved, before we accepted Him, and yes, even before we walked in relationship with Him--*He died for us.* Before we were even thinking about Him, *He had already died.* God, the Father, through the man Jesus Christ, had already made up His mind long ago that **He would choose us. My God!** *He consented to receive **and** undertake us **by** His **acceptance** of us through Jesus' death on the cross.* Philippians 2:5-8 NKJV says, "**5** Let this mind be in you which was also in Christ Jesus, **6** who, being in the form of God, did not consider it robbery to be equal with God, **7** but made Himself of no reputation, taking the form of a bondservant, *and* coming in the likeness of men. **8** And being found in appearance as a man, He humbled Himself and became obedient to the point of death, even the death of the cross." This scripture reveals to us that Jesus, in His divinity, humbled Himself and served us through His death--choosing us before we even had a mind to receive or choose Him.

1 John 4:8 NKJV says, "He who does not love does not know God, for **God is love**." The part I want to focus on is that God is love. He loved us enough to pursue us in our adamic nature; in the very nature that was enmity to Him, in the very nature that "rubbed Him" the wrong way...*He chose love; He chose consent; He chose acceptance.* 1 John 4:9-10 NKJV goes on to say, "In this the love of God was manifested towards us, that God sent His only begotten Son into the world, that we might live through Him. In this is love, not that we loved God, but that He loved us and sent His Son to be the propitiation for our sins." My Pastor frequently quotes John 3:16 and recites it as "For God so loved the world that He **gave...**" Jesus made His love manifest to us by giving the only thing that could remit our sins and make us right with Him--*Himself.*

Love

It's essential to take a closer look at what love is while we are on the topic of God being the very epitome of love. Firstly, when talking about love, it's worth noting that love is one of the fruit of the Spirit. In its original Greek language meaning agapē, love is affection, good will, benevolence, and a form of brotherly love. In 1 John 4, the Apostle John speaks about love in profound formalities. 1 John 4: 7-8, 10 NKJV reads:

7 Beloved, let us love one another, <u>for love is of God</u>; and everyone who loves is born of God and knows God.

8 He who does not love does not know God, <u>for God is love</u>.

10 <u>In this is love,</u> **not that we loved God, but that He loved us and sent His Son to be the propitiation for our sins.**

God is love, and this is love: that he loved us and sent His Son to be the atonement for our sins. God is the standard of what love is. *Love is Him and Him? Well--love.*

Given this, this means that we could conclude that because love is a fruit of the Spirit and because Jesus is Spirit and the Truth (John 4:24; John 14:6, 7, 17, 26; John 15:26). Everything that the Bible declares to be love, Jesus is and has been towards us--*His creation of whom He has entirely accepted and committed Himself to.* What a unique concept to grab ahold of: the God of the universe has chosen to spend eternity investing in us as His children. *Jesus!*

What does this mean more directly, you wonder? Well, first, let's read about what the Bible says love is. One of the most well-known and referenced scriptures that describes love is found in 1 Corinthians 13. 1 Corinthians 13:4-8 NKJV reads:

4 Love suffers long *and* is kind; love does not envy; love does not parade itself, is not puffed up;

5 does not behave rudely, does not seek its own, is not provoked, thinks no evil;

6 does not rejoice in iniquity, but rejoices in the truth;

7 bears all things, believes all things, hopes all things, endures all things.

8 **Love never fails.** But whether *there are* prophecies, they will fail; whether *there are* tongues, they will cease; whether *there is* knowledge, it will vanish away.

These scriptures are prophesying and speaking of the very thing that God is: love.

What does this mean for the believer today? This understanding means that concerning us, Jesus is:

- **long-suffering** or patient,

- He is **kind**,

- He is **not** envious of nor towards us,

- He **does not** parade Himself (boastful) or is **not** puffed up, proud, or prideful,

- He **does not** behave rudely towards us,

- He **does not** seek His own, is self-seeking, or selfish,

- He is **not easily** provoked,

- He thinks **no** evil concerning us,

- He **does not** rejoice in iniquity concerning us but instead rejoices in truth,

- He **bears all things, believes all things, hopes all things, endures all things**, and

- Lastly, His love towards us **NEVER fails**

If I could sum all of this up for you, I would say that: God--*Jesus* loved us enough to be accepting of us--*giving us Himself even in the presence of our fleshly nature rearing its ugly head.* **What a Wonderful, Mighty God that we serve!**

Now, what does this mean for us today, you may wonder? Well, firstly, it points to the fact that we can only love God because He first loved us (1 John 4:19 KJV). So what do we do after He initiates (which He has already done, by the way, through His death)? **We receive His love for us** because only in us receiving His love can we truly, genuinely, and sincerely love Him properly (with truth, genuineness, and sincerity as the foundation of our love). We, in return, accept His love for us; we *consent to His love for us*. In other words, even though we are imperfect beings (*and will get it "wrong" more than once*), we consent to receive and steward His love that was extended to us despite our imperfection. Our response to Him accepting us through love is us receiving His acceptance of us; by us receiving His love, we automatically embrace His acceptance of us.

My main encouragement to you in this chapter is to: **let Jesus love you.** When noticing the sinful nature of our flesh, it's easier to be hard on ourselves. But in those moments, it is best to allow room for Him to love us even more. His love washes, it cleans, it whitens, it purifies; therefore, when we notice the works of the flesh, Love (Jesus) is the conduit to our purification amid fleshy works. We must not hide from or deny His purifying work (through love) when we are confronted with the lusts of the flesh. Accepting Jesus' love for you while walking in a lifestyle of Grace over perfection is simply being able to let yourself go enough to allow yourself to be loved by Him in your flaws and imperfections--knowing that He **wants** to love you. He **desires** to love you in that **very** place...That very tension that you're struggling in; **the tension of the flesh (the adamic nature) vs. the spirit (the new, redeemed nature).** [For me, the tension I was living in was seeing the works of the flesh manifesting (jealousy, envy, and comparison) when I wasn't pursuing the works of the flesh]. *Jesus* does not want you to seek Him or only come to Him when you think you have it all together (only He can **truly** be a determiner of that anyway), but in those moments when you think you don't, *as well.*

Early September of 2019, in the spirit of revisiting the words from the therapist that cool-breezed, Summer morning in July. I found myself sharing with the Lord how I desired to be more accepting of others and more forgiving in light of who they are. *Go figure.* And as I confessed my desires to the

Lord, He immediately reminded me that if I am not accepting and forgiving others, then somewhere along the line, I'm not accepting, forgiving, and being loving towards *myself*. Uh oh. But, you know what? After several months of walking through intensive healing, I handled this situation a little differently--more like that of a Daughter, *a son of God, and not that of an orphan*. Needless to say, I didn't freak out because I didn't perceive me desiring to work on a certain area in my life as a threat to who I am or whose I am, for that matter. I more easily walked into this with the Lord. I asked myself, "Why? Why am I not accepting and forgiving towards myself?" I did some backtracking, taking a look into my past experiences. As a detective following his footsteps to engage in the breakthrough of his case, I fearlessly looked back.

A journal entry from September 4, 2019-(edited for the sake of this book):

> "I saw my mistakes as a reason why people couldn't or shouldn't love me--as if my mistakes deemed me unlovable. And with God, I saw it as a reason why He couldn't invest in me or continue to work on me further; I saw my mistakes as a disqualifier [to receive His perfect love for me]. [I realize though], God isn't looking for me to be perfect to love me with His **best** love. [What this means for my God-given relationships today is that] I don't have to desire others to be perfect before I decide that I am going to love them. Furthermore, I intentionally and sacrificially decide to pursue [relationship with] them

in the way that Jesus is/has called(ing) me to [and even in the way that He did for me]. [James 4:14 NKJV enlightens me that, "...whereas you do not know what will happen tomorrow, **For what is your life? It is even a vapor that appears for a little time then vanishes away.**" My life is but a vapor; it appears for a little time then vanishes away. Who am I to decide how or when I will love someone based on how *I feel* they love me or even how I *feel* about *the way* that they love or treat me. Did Jesus look to my actions to see if I was worthy of being loved? **No!** And I'm sure if He did, I would have been out of luck. That humbles me. I don't get to decide when, who, or how I will show mercy, love, or forgiveness--it's a given. Plus, not even that, Jesus didn't wait before He chose to love me. He made up His mind and **loved** me out of the **practicing** of my sinful, adamic nature. He didn't wait until I was 'perfect' because if He did, I would have nothing going for me in regard to receiving His love]."

The Bible says, in Romans 13:8 NKJV, to, "Owe no one anything except to love one another, for he who loves another has fulfilled the law." Therefore, if I am having a hard time loving someone, I must first look at how I am receiving (*and if I have fully accepted*) the Lord's love in the area of my life that I am struggling to love someone else in. I had to understand that His love for me (despite my flaws) was perfect; it is whole; it is complete concerning me. So I encourage you with this today: look at what God *did* for the born again believer; *look at how He accepted you and consented to **all that you are and will be.*** Isaiah 43:1-7 NKJV says,

> "But now, thus says the Lord, who **created** you, O Jacob,
>
> And He who **formed** you, O Israel:
>
> 'Fear not, for I have **redeemed** you;
>
> I have **called** *you* by your name;
>
> **You** *are* Mine. When you pass through the waters, I *will be* with you; And through the rivers, they shall not overflow you.
>
> When you walk through the fire, you shall not be burned,
>
> Nor shall the flame scorch you. For I *am* the Lord your God,
>
> The Holy One of Israel, your Savior;
>
> I **gave** Egypt for your ransom,
>
> Ethiopia and Seba in your place. Since you were precious in My sight, You have been honored,
>
> And I have **loved** you;

Therefore I will **give** men for you,

And people for your life. Fear not, for I *am* with you;

I will bring your descendants from the east,

And gather you from the west; I will say to the north,'
'Give them up!' And to the south, 'Do not keep them
back!'

'Bring My sons from afar,

And My daughters from the ends of the earth—
Everyone who is called by My name, whom I have
created for My glory;

I have **formed** him, yes, I have **made** him.'"

I love this particular passage. Look at what the Lord did
for **you.** He created; formed; redeemed; called; gave; loved,
and made **you.** If you haven't fully understood it at this
point: the Lord's love is **faithful** and **unconditional**
concerning His children. For His love to be faithful means
that it is trustworthy (dependable and reliable); full of trust--it
is sure. Conditions do not limit the unconditional love of
God; it is absolute--full, perfect, and whole. His love is free of
flaws and is without spot, wrinkle, or blemish. Let me put
this as plain as I can: God's love is **trustworthy, dependable,**
reliable, unconditional (not limited by conditions),
complete, perfect, without spot, or blemish, free from
restriction or limitation, it is positive and certain

concerning you. In other words, God has not and is not giving up on you; He has committed who He is to love you; He has made you accepted in the beloved (Ephesians 1:6 KJV).

Back to me early September of 2019.

1 John 4:18 NKJV says, "There is no fear in love; but perfect love casts out fear, because fear involves torment. But he who fears has not been made perfect in love." What this revealed to me is that if I questioned if my mistakes still allowed me in the beloved--I was operating in the spirit of fear. If I questioned Him remaining in relationship with me based on if I was behaving perfectly or not, indeed, it points to me being fearful of Him leaving, giving up on, or abandoning me. To take it a step further, this then revealed that I still needed to be made perfect, mature, or made whole-complete in this area of my life. I needed to see Him as my Father, Who loved me not because of what I did but because of who He is in His committing to love me.

You see now?

The problem was that not being accepting of others pointed to my lack of accepting and being forgiving of myself. In return, this ultimately pointed to the areas in my life where I needed to receive (by way of acceptance) Christ's love for me so that I can then be accepting of others. There was an order to this stronghold, and it started with me receiving Christ's *pure* love for me. I needed to receive Christ's love for me in this area so that I could be positioned to accept and be forgiving towards myself, **and then**, *eventually, others (we'll get there later).*

Living a lifestyle of Grace over Perfection: *Acceptance*

One may ask: Well, LaGerrica, I understand what you wrote about walking in the acceptance of the Lord's love for me, **but** *how do I do it practically?*

Accepting Jesus' love for you, allowing for His perfect love to cast out all fear in you, is a process and isn't something that happens overnight. We truly learn it as we walk this walk, and sometimes we fall back into the mindset of fear and not accepting the Lord's love and, thus, need His Grace to pull us back in. However, I do believe that the main ingredient one needs to accept the Lord's love for them is-- dependence on Him. Read this:

- When Jesus preached His first sermon on the mount (known as The Beatitudes) recorded in Matthew 5:1 NKJV, the first thing He said was, "Blessed are the poor in spirit, For theirs is the kingdom of heaven."

- Psalm 51:17 NKJV says, "The sacrifices of God are a broken spirit, A broken and a contrite heart-These, O God, You will not despise."

- Psalm 34:18 KJV says, "The Lord is nigh unto them that are of a broken heart; and saveth such as be of a contrite spirit."

Each one of these scriptures speaks of God honoring, delivering, and rewarding the one with a broken spirit and a contrite heart. Why? Because the one who is broken and contrite before God depends *on Him when and if they get past themselves enough to do so.*

You see, when we are having a hard time accepting the Lord's love, it's not because we don't want to, but it's because there is some kind of tension that we are living in that's stopping us from doing so. Let me explain. When I was struggling with the works of the flesh: overwhelming thoughts of jealousy, envy, and comparison, it caused me to doubt my identity in God, and I couldn't properly accept Christ's love for me. Remember that it's Christ's love that purifies and cleanses us from unrighteousness. The devil loves more than anything to keep us bound in our flesh, ignorant of the fact that we have access to Grace and the Lord's love that sets us free.

Naturally, my acknowledgment of my sinful thoughts (along with my desire to not own them) put me in the state of a broken spirit and a contrite heart; I wanted to accept God's love, His Grace--His mercy. I had no choice but to depend on Him while He matured me in the understanding I needed to grow in His love. It was in my reliance on God that I accepted His love for me even while working out my own salvation (Philippians 2:12 NKJV). I had to trust in His acceptance of me when I didn't even accept myself; this trust birthed a genuine relationship with God. I had to believe what the Lord said about me more than what my actions and thoughts were saying. More than the lies of the enemy, and even more than my judgments against me. Dependence brought me through; dependence helped to heal me; dependence gave me hope because, without dependence, I couldn't have matured in God's love.

So now you see, accepting His love starts with dependence on Him. Depending on His love for you even while striving to get everything right but realizing *you simply can't.* His grace is sufficient, and His power is made perfect (mature, complete) in our weaknesses, according to 2 Corinthians 12:9 NKJV.

CHAPTER 5

ɞ

Love God

"'You shall love the Lord your God *with all your heart, with all your soul, and with all your strength.* And these words which I command you today shall be in your heart. You shall teach them diligently to your children, and shall talk of them when you sit in your house, when you walk by the way, when you lie down, and when you rise up.'" ~Deuteronomy 6:5-7 NKJV

In Matthew 22:23-33 NKJV--to set the scene--Jesus has just finished giving divine revelation about the resurrection to the Sadducees, and the Bible says that they were astonished.

So by the time that verses 34-36 come around, one of the Pharisees, who is a lawyer (after hearing that Jesus silenced the Sadducees) asks Jesus a question, the Bible says, to tempt Him. He asked, "Master, which is the great commandment in the law?" I think it's worth noting that all the Pharisees cared about was keeping the law that Moses commanded the children of Israel. The Bible explains the Pharisees' as people who trusted in themselves and despised others; all they *truly* cared about was keeping the law and validating themselves and their status by how well they kept the law. *They even judged themselves to be better or more esteemed because of how well they kept the law.* In Luke 18:9-14 NKJV, Jesus shared a parable that mirrors an example of the Pharisees' way of thinking in how they viewed themselves, in comparison to others:

> "9 **Also He spoke this parable to some who trusted in themselves that they were righteous, and despised others**: 10 Two men went up to the temple to pray, one a Pharisee and the other a tax collector. 11 The Pharisee stood and prayed thus with himself, 'God, I thank You that I am not like other men— extortioners, unjust, adulterers, or even as this tax collector. 12 I fast twice a week; I give tithes of all that I possess.' 13 And the tax collector, standing afar off, would not so much as raise *his* eyes to heaven, but beat his breast, saying, 'God, be merciful to me a sinner!' 14 I tell you, this man went down to his house justified *rather* than the other; *for everyone who exalts himself will be humbled, and he who humbles himself will be exalted.*"

As you can see, the Pharisees had a way of esteeming and justifying themselves in a way that wasn't a picture of God's valid justification, but rather their justification; *they valued themselves based on their works.* If we carefully and rightly analyzed their mindset and behavior, the Pharisees possessed a form of the mindset that was rooted in that of an orphan child that we talked about in Chapter one. They looked to their works and what they could do *for* Christ to validate themselves *in* Him rather than looking to Him, loving Him with all of their heart, and allowing their faith in Him to justify and validate (Romans 3:28 KJV) them. So anyway, now that we know that, let's get back to Matthew 22!

Jesus responds in verses 37, 38 saying, "'You shall love the Lord your God with all your heart, with all your soul, and with all your mind. This is *the* first and great commandment.'" *Do you see this?!* When the Pharisee asked what the great commandment in the law was, Jesus quoted Deuteronomy 6; to love the Lord your God with all your heart, soul, and with all your strength (*or mind*). *Loving the Lord, our God, with all of our **hearts, souls, and minds** is the very first and great commandment and reveals to us how we ought to love God.* It also foresees how we are to receive His love (which is learned before healthily loving Him and comes before we can love ourselves in wholeness, and thus, loving our neighbor healthily). We will get into this more in-depth further in this book.

Let's take a look at Matthew 22:37, 38 more closely.

Love the Lord your God with all your: *heart*

The heart. It's such a **powerful** organ! Beating around 100,000 times a day, the heart weighs less than one pound and can continue beating *even* when it's disconnected from the body. Wow! What a special, essential organ to the human body. This interesting fact is why we could find it surprising when the prophet Jeremiah says in Jeremiah 17:9 KJV, "The heart is deceitful above all things, And desperately wicked; Who can know it?" What? The organ that keeps our bodies alive is desperately wicked? How can this be? Another phrase for desperately wicked is incurably sick. Our hearts are deceitful above all things and incurably sick--so much so that no one can know it *(well, no one except for Jesus). That seems so deep, doesn't it?* Almost like there's no point of return for our hearts. Why does God want us to love Him with all of what seems so filthy? How can the heart be such a pivotal organ to "life" in our bodies but in the same breath be the same thing that makes us incurably sick, *spiritually*? **This concept is worth looking into further.**

Our hearts reflect our experiences, what we choose to allow to feed us (TV, music, books, etc.), the places we decide to hang, the company we desire and decide to keep, and more! The heart harbors all of these things, and given the broken world we live in, *Jesus knows this.* So He warns us that our heart is the first thing that harbors the brokenness of this world, amongst other things (i.e., the principles of God, etc.). The Bible tells us that, out of the heart flows the issues of life (Proverbs 4:23b). Our will, what we commit to, comes from the heart first and then flows to our thought life, *or our minds*, where we then choose to commit to an action; and so Jesus says, "You know what...just give me your heart, surrender it to me, love me with **all** of it--so that I can transform it, change it, put my ways, my desires, and my will in it." Allow Him to be the main driving force of your heart, causing you to walk in His ways. Because here's the truth-- *our hearts are only made right with **<u>Him residing in them</u>***. He has to be Lord over our hearts for them to produce any good thing.

Therefore, *with this in mind*, the Lord instructs us in Proverbs 4:23 NKJV to:

"<u>Keep your heart with all diligence,</u>

For out of it *spring* the issues of life."

The word 'keep' here, in the original Hebrew, is natsar and means to guard, to protect, and to preserve; we keep and protect our heart because the Word says that out of it spring the issues of life. God looks at the heart and man, the outward appearance; 1 Samuel 16:7 NKJV says, "But the Lord said to Samuel, 'Do not look at his appearance or at his physical stature, because I have refused him. For *the Lord does* not *see* as man sees; for man looks at the outward appearance, but **the Lord** looks at the heart.'" When the prophet Samuel was seeking the king that the Lord sought to anoint for Israel, he went to Jesse's home, and after having seven of his sons pass before Samuel, the Lord told Samuel that none of them are who He has chosen to be king. And when Samuel asked if

Jesse has any more sons, King David (although he wasn't king yet) was invited in and anointed king. David, in the Bible, is known as a seeker of God's heart; his heart was pure and was in a continual state of cleansing before the Lord. That particular day, God desired and sought who had a pure heart before him.

So when we think about how to love God with all of our hearts, we seek His heart and the intents of His heart molds into **ours,** *by the Grace of God.* Psalm 37:4 NKJV says, "Delight yourself also in the Lord, And He shall give you the desires of your heart." The Lord gives us the desires of our hearts because as we delight ourselves in Him, He gives us His desires for us. In the same way, when we position ourselves to seek the Lord's heart, His heart's desire eventually becomes ours. Our hearts are *truly* incurably sick without God being in control.

Here are some scriptures and essential information that we could meditate on to understand the importance of **keeping** our hearts pure before the Lord (they act as a summary of what I've already been writing). A heart that is tainted with things that are contrary to God cannot follow His commands (John 14:15 NKJV) while fully and truly love Him the way He desires:

- **Proverbs 27:19** NKJV says, "As in water face reflects face, So a man's heart reveals the man." Our hearts reflect our meditative thoughts. It reflects unresolved experiences, past hurts, pains, etc.; our hearts harbor these things, and if we are not careful, they can reside in us, infect us, and eventually will reflect the condition that our hearts lie in.

- **Matthew 6:21** NKJV says, "For where your treasure is, there your heart will be also." What you focus on, meditate on, consume your time with--whatever you put your treasure in, your heart will reside. Furthermore, if your heart isn't living in things that are pleasing before God and edifying to your relationship with Him--your treasure will be in vain activities.

- **Proverbs 15:13** NKJV says, "A merry heart makes a cheerful countenance, but by sorrow of the heart the spirit is broken." The heart can influence and reveal the condition that we are in mentally, spiritually, and even emotionally.

- **John 7:38** NKJV says, "He who believes in Me, as the Scripture has said, out of his heart will flow rivers of living water." What resides in our hearts will flow out so much that our belief in Him can cause rivers of living water to flow out of our hearts (not only when we are filled with His Spirit, but generally speaking, as well).

- We not only love God with all our hearts, but we trust Him with it, as well. **Proverbs 3:5-7** NKJV says, "5 **Trust in the Lord with all your heart**, and lean not on your own understanding; 6 In all your ways acknowledge Him, And He shall direct your paths. 7

Do not be wise in your own eyes; fear the Lord and depart from evil."

- What we spend our time doing will eventually begin to flow out of our hearts. This understanding is why it is very important to be careful and picky about what we allow in our inner man because it could affect us in ways that we do not bargain for them to. **Matthew 12:34** NKJV says, "Brood of vipers! How can you, being evil, speak good things? For out of the abundance of the heart the mouth speaks."

Love the Lord your God with all your heart, with all your *soul*

As I mentioned before, our souls are made up of our mind, will, and emotions. The first time that we see the word 'soul' in the Bible is pretty early on in Genesis 2:7 KJV which says, "And the Lord God formed man of the dust of the ground, and breathed into his nostrils the breath of life; and man became a living **soul**." In the original Hebrew language, the word soul here means *nephesh.* According to the Blue Letter Bible, the soul is translated using words like **life, person, mind, heart, creature,** and **body.** The way that the Bible uses the word 'soul' can be described as *soul, self, life, creature, person, appetite, mind, living being, desire, emotion, and passion; thus meaning:*

- that which breathes, the breathing substance or being, soul, the inner being of man
- living being

- living being (with life in the blood)

- the man himself, self, person or individual

- the seat of the appetites

- the seat of emotions and passions

- the activity of the mind

  o Dubious; meaning, *hesitating and doubting; not to be relied upon; suspect.*

- the activity of the will

  o Dubious

- the activity of the character

  o Dubious

Because our souls are the house of all of these different functions, we have to be sure that they are healed and healthy. We need our souls to be healthy and healed in the sight of God so that the things we have an appetite for are pleasing before God and in alignment with His will for our lives. For example, this can include the overall convictions of the church as a body (i.e., adultery, fornication, uncleanness, idolatry, and anything else the Lord instructs the church in through His Word). This example can also include the individual convictions of each believer. For instance, this can include not watching certain TV shows and movies, not partaking in certain kinds of activities, choosing not to wear certain clothes, etc.. When a believer is born again, the Lord can give them convictions that He doesn't give others; *this is what I'm referring to by individual convictions.* The danger of an unhealthy soul is the possibility of committing to a life that is not pleasing to the Lord. You can begin to desire and lust after things He does not have for **you**; you can participate in things He doesn't desire for **you**--in activities that He isn't in, *which ultimately separates you from Him.* This distraction is surely what the enemy, Satan, wants.

The truth is: a *tainted soul is a soul far from God,* **even when we partake in spiritual activities.** Today, one of the dangers of the church is participating in religious activities, services, and "revivals" that God is not in, *even though it looks like He is.* As born again believers, we must be careful in discerning how we respond to these kinds of activities Here's the central reason: it's not because spiritual operations, practices, and services in and of themselves aren't pleasing before the Lord. *Instead, it's the souls and motives behind those who are leading them.* What is the spiritual condition of the soul(s) leading it, the soul who is speaking at it? At times, I don't think we ask ourselves these questions. Nevertheless, the matter remains that an unhealthy soul, one that is contrary to God, one that is separate from God, is a tainted soul. My dearly, Beloved-Friend, tainted souls cannot lead to **effective** revivals, services, or spiritual activities.

At this point in the chapter, one may be considering how we ought to keep our souls in a healthy condition before the sight of the Lord; I'm glad you asked. Well, next to following the individual convictions that the Holy Spirit has given us, we must also **hear** the sayings and instructions of the Lord and **do** them. In other words, we must spend time with the Lord through His Word to learn His instruction for our lives as a body and as an individual and **do them**. Matthew 7:24-27 NKJV says,

> "Therefore whoever **hears** these sayings of Mine, and **does** them, I will liken him to a wise man who built his house on the rock: and the rain descended, the floods came, and the winds blew and beat on that house; and it did not fall, for it was founded on the rock. 'But everyone who **hears** these sayings of Mine, and **does not do them**, will be like a foolish man who built his house on the sand: and the rain descended, the floods came, and the winds blew and beat on that house; and it fell. *And great was its fall.*'"

The scriptures speak of two kinds of people: those who hear Jesus' sayings and do them and those who hear them and do not do them (also remember Mark 4:20 KJV and James 1:22-24 NKJV). When we hear and do the sayings of the Lord--when we keep His commandments, we not only keep our souls healthy but we also are like a wise man that built his house upon the Rock that stands the time of tests, trials, tribulations, and storms. Don't mistake what I am saying here, *Jesus is the Rock.* Not to mention, to keep the soul healthy, one must walk in the Spirit; you must be so full of Christ that you may know Him and the power of his resurrection, and the fellowship of His sufferings, being made conformable unto His death (Philippians 3:10 NKJV). Also, that you refrain from sowing seeds to your flesh; Galatians 6:7-9 NKJV says,

> "7 Do not be deceived, God is not mocked; for whatever a man sows, that he will also reap. 8 For he who sows to his flesh will of the **flesh reap corruption**, but he who sows to the **Spirit will of the Spirit reap everlasting life.** 9 And let us not grow weary while doing good, for in due season we shall reap if we do not lose heart."

When we partake in things that the Lord does not desire us to, we are sowing seeds to our flesh, which is in-return tainting our souls. However, when we sow seeds to the Spirit, we are planting seeds into eternal, everlasting life with our Savior. When sowing seeds to the Spirit, we are renewing and refreshing our souls in the Spirit of God.

I would advise that at this point in this chapter that you would take some time to examine yourself. 2 Corinthians 5:7 NKJV says, "Examine yourselves *as to* whether you are in the faith. Test yourselves. Do you not know yourselves, that Jesus Christ is in you?—unless indeed you are disqualified." Because this isn't a topic that ministers frequently teach on, we should take some time to examine ourselves before God today. Think about the condition of your soul. *Is it healthy? Is it tainted? Is it barely functioning? Is it pleasing before God?* These questions are not to ridicule you but to get you in a place where you're honest with God and thus honest with yourself.

Love the Lord your God with all your heart, with all your soul, and with all your *mind*

When considering our minds, one of the first things that the Lord revealed to me is that the mind depicts **the decisions and posture of our hearts.** Therefore, what we set our hearts upon we have chosen to fix our minds upon. This revelation is why the decision and commitment of our minds reveal to us the posture--commitment, decision, and stance of our hearts. In Numbers 16:28 KJV Moses says (as he's speaking to the children of Israel), "And Moses said, Hereby ye shall know that the LORD hath sent me to do all these works; for *I have* not *done them* of mine own **mind**." Essentially Moses is saying that I have not done these things or actions because of *my* **decision** that became my own capabilities. *This reflection is important because it displays to us that Moses is speaking of his mind in the same way that he is speaking of committing to a decision, physically.*

Colossians 3:2 KJV instructs us to, "**Set your affection** on things above, not on things on the earth." The part of the scripture I want us to focus on is the phrase 'set your affection.' The phrase 'set your affection' in the original Greek is *phroneō,* in which the outline of Biblical usage means [according to the Blue Letter Bible] to direct one's mind to a thing, to seek, and to strive for. It also points to *exercising the mind and being mentally disposed, earnestly, in a certain direction.* So when the Apostle Paul said to the church of Colossi to "set your affection on things above," he was surely telling them to set their **minds** on things above. I share this to simply say, **where your affection--where your heart is set, *there is where your mind is resting upon, as well.***

If we are going to walk with Christ, be committed to Him, and love Him with all of our minds--we have to set our affections, or our minds on Him so that our decisions are pure. And you know what? There's a sweet and kind promise to the one who keeps their mind stayed on Him. Isaiah 26:3 NKJV says, "You will keep *him* in perfect peace, *whose* mind *is* stayed *on You,* Because he trusts in You." The Lord will keep us in perfect peace when our minds are stay on Him because the Lord loves for us to trust in Him; not only this, but a mind stayed on Him is a mind that remains pure. Don't you want a mind that's *stayed* on Him?

Further, this is also why it is crucial for us as born again believers to be careful of what we set our minds on, aka what we **think** about and what we allow our minds to rest on. What we set our minds on, we will eventually choose to commit to doing those things. The Apostle Paul, in Philippians 4:8 NKJV, instructs, "Finally, brethren, whatever things are true, whatever things *are* noble, whatever things *are* just, whatever things *are* pure, whatever things *are* lovely, whatever things *are* of good report, if *there is* any virtue and if *there is* anything praiseworthy—meditate on these things." We meditate on things that are true, noble, just, etc. because if we set our mind on things opposite, we sacrifice a healthy soul, and the danger with this is that an unhealthy soul equals an unhealthy **mind.**

I have compiled some scriptures about the importance of our mind below:

- Romans 8:5-6 NKJV: "5 For those who live according to the flesh set their minds on the things of the flesh, but those *who live* according to the Spirit, the things of the Spirit. 6 For to be carnally minded *is* death, but to be spiritually minded *is* life and peace."

- Romans 12:1-2 NKJV: "1 I beseech you therefore, brethren, by the mercies of God, that you present your bodies a living sacrifice, holy, acceptable to God, *which is* your reasonable service. 2 And do not be conformed to this world, but be transformed by the renewing of your mind, that you may prove what *is* that good and acceptable and perfect will of God."

- 2 Corinthians 10:5 NKJV: "5 casting down arguments and every high thing that exalts itself against the knowledge of God, bringing every thought into captivity to the obedience of Christ,"

- 2 Timothy 1:7 NKJV: "7 For God has not given us a spirit of fear, but of power and of love and of a sound mind."

- Philippians 2:5 NKJV: "5 Let this mind be in you which was also in Christ Jesus,"

The matter concludes that to love God with all of your heart, soul, and mind, you have to have a surrendered heart, soul, and mind to the Lord. He has to have full control and free will over those areas of our lives because, without His hand in those areas, we are likely to be walking around with tainted hearts. Still saved, still attending services, still having revivals but all along carrying a tainted heart and soul (mind, will, and emotions). This circumstance is dangerous to the bride of Christ; we have to keep these areas in check. I love the order in which Jesus said to love Him: first with your heart, soul, and then your mind. Because the heart speaks to and drives the soul, mind, will, and emotions. It all starts with the heart. King David prayed, "Create in me a clean heart, O God, And renew a steadfast spirit within me" (Psalm 51:10 NKJV). David knew something that we ought to know--*that for a soul (in the way I've been speaking of it) to thrive in God,* **our hearts** *must be cleansed and surrendered unto the will of the Father.*

I want to share something else with you. In Psalm 139, verses 1-18 are spent with David sharing His love and adoration to God for being an infinite Father who created all of mankind. However, by the time verse 19-22 comes around the tone of the Psalmist switched, and David stated:

19 "Oh, that You would slay the wicked, O God!

Depart from me, therefore, you bloodthirsty men.

20 For they speak against You wickedly; Your enemies take *Your name* in vain.

21 Do I not hate them, O Lord, who hate You?

And do I not loathe those who rise up against You?

22 I hate them with perfect hatred; I count them my enemies."

But then David's tone calms again in verses 23 and 24, and he says:

23 "Search me, O God, and know my heart;

Try me, and know my anxieties;

24 And see if *there is any* wicked way in me,

And lead me in the way everlasting."

David went from being aggressive in verses 19-22 to asking the Lord to search His heart (verses 23-24). I believe this is because David realized that in the same way that those who are wicked possess tainted, wicked hearts, *so does he.* David had understood that within him and in his heart lies the same ability to have the same posture that can cause him to be just as wicked as those of whom he was speaking of in verses 19-22. He realized that without God searching, knowing, and trying his heart, his heart could be in the same wicked state as those whom he'd declared wicked.

I reiterate once more that we must realize, too, that to thrive in God, having a healthy relationship with Christ, loving Him with all of our heart, soul, and mind-these things need to be surrendered to Him, *the one who can cleanse and make them pleasing before Him.* Let's invite the Lord to cleanse us today that we may not be deceived but rather walk with Him in Spirit and Truth.

CHAPTER 6

&

Love Yourself

"And the second is like unto it, Thou shalt love thy neighbor as thyself. On these two commandments hang all the law and the prophets." ~Matthew 22:39-40 KJV

One day, in late October of 2019, I found myself at the altar during Sunday service at my church, I found myself at the altar during the middle of service. This particular day I'd genuinely realized how sinful my flesh *is. I mean, I'd carried a level of understanding before but this day, I'd understood it in a new way.* A way that made me repent and had me worshipping God at the altar as *I needed what felt like closeness and a one-on-one encounter with the King in that present moment.*

After we've received the Lord's love for us [while pursuing a lifestyle of Grace over perfection] and are now loving Him back, it is now time to pursue a lifestyle of loving ourselves.

Not just in any ordinary way, but *the way the Lord loves us and deems us to love ourselves*. This is *soon to come* next after we've committed ourselves to love God.

You see, there is a difference between loving yourself in your strength and in loving and seeing yourself through the lens of the Lord. The world would tell you that loving yourself is found from within--that for one to love themselves, they have to 'find' love from the inside (*as if True Love could be found in these mortal, fleshly bodies without them redeemed by Christ*). *However, what do you expect the world to tell you?* It could only give you what it has--a false representation of love. Love is **not** found from the inside without Christ, and if we commit our time to love ourselves the world's way, we commit ourselves to fall short every time. We commit to going in endless cycles, wanting to love ourselves, but not possessing what we need to do this in a fulfilling way. How would you prefer to love yourself? With your strength, with the world's, or with the Lord's?

Before Christ, there were plenty of times where I had tried to take the world's model of what it meant for me to love myself and use it to help me be content with the way God had created me. Since a young girl, I've always been a thicker, chocolate (darker-skinned), young lady. Realizing early that this wasn't the world's standard of beauty, I tried everything I could to force myself to believe that I was beautiful--that I was worth *something*, that I was valuable. *Trying to believe that within me was a love for myself that would sustain my insecurities.* But the truth is that without Christ, I was never going to find this, and I never did *until I encountered Him.*

When the Lord saved me, in His timing, I had started to learn what it looked like for me to love myself in Him; to learn that my love for me adapts *from* His love for me. I had to learn that my love for myself *isn't* separate from His love for me, but rather, my "self-love" is **found in His love for me.** There's a difference between the two, you know. Because if we truly want to love ourselves the way we were intended to, according to God's will, then we understand that our love for ourselves houses in something greater than us—in His love for us. And you know what else? We have to accept His love for us. Because in our acceptance of His love for us **is** our love for ourselves.

So, what does it look like to love yourself? As I mentioned before, the world would tell us that it's believing in yourself, or it's found within, or even that it's something that is formed or concurred by you. *What a false narrative and danger this is for the born again believer to adapt to.* Because the truth is: in and of ourselves, we do not have what it takes to love ourselves, in the same way that we don't have what it takes to save ourselves.

1 John 4:9 KJV says, "**In this was manifested the love of God toward us**, because that God sent His only begotten Son into the world, that we might live through Him." This understanding, here, is the way that salvation is made available to us. However, I present to you that also here is the key ingredient to one loving themselves the way that God

does; that we may love others with a love that doesn't come from ourselves but comes from God *(we'll get into that later though)*. The key ingredient to the born again believer loving themselves the way the Lord does is found in God sending His only begotten Son into the world, that we might live through Him. This truth **is** what loving yourself is for the believer; *it's found in the Son's sacrifice for sinful people.* As I slightly mentioned before and if you'd allow me to say it more directly: His love **toward** us **is our love for ourselves.**

Loving ourselves is found after we love Him back. After all, after we love Him back, we have a healthy look at what it looks like to love in a Godly manner because we have witnessed God's love so deeply, personally, and intimately. *Once you love Him back, Jesus positions you to love yourself as He loves you.*

Saved from the Pharisee Mindset

While looking more deeply at this topic, outside of the world's way of advising one to love themselves, I realized that there is another barrier to us loving ourselves in Christ, the way He's called us to. And it's this concept: if His love towards us is our love for ourselves and His passion **was** God sending "His only begotten Son into the world, that we might live through Him," then what could stop or hinder us from loving ourselves **is in** the way we perceive the Lord's sacrifice in our lives; in how 'weighty' and 'impactful' we are allowing His sacrifice to be in our lives; how **BIG** we are making His sacrifice in our lives.

In other words, if we are not delivered from the orphan or the Pharisee mindset [that deceitfully says our acceptance in Christ is found in how perfect we are or how "well" we do things in Him], then we will continuously be hindered from seeing the fullness and beauty of His sacrifice for us. We will fail to understand the beauty of our need and dependence on Him. *Hmmm, child of God, this is so important to understand.* If we don't allow Jesus to deliver us from the orphan/Pharisee mindset, then we can't truly love ourselves the way God intended us to. Likewise, loving ourselves is birthed when the Lord delivers us from the Pharisee/orphan child mindset.

More intently, we've talked about the mindset of the Pharisees in Chapter five, but I would like to touch on it more deeply. The Pharisees and teachers of the law were much so only concerned with how perfectly they followed the law that a relationship with Jesus wasn't their main concern. One could say that to them, their works or deeds were their relationships with God. To them, they should have been more esteemed because they were "more perfect" than everyone else. **This mindset prevented them from seeing the Savior when He was flesh and blood, right there in their faces.** They couldn't see the Savior because they weren't in tune with their **need** for the Savior.

Luke 7:37-48 NKJV says:

> "**37** And behold, a woman in the city who was a sinner, when she knew that *Jesus* sat at the table in the Pharisee's house, brought an alabaster flask of fragrant oil, **38** and stood at His feet behind *Him* weeping; and

she began to wash His feet with her tears, and wiped *them* with the hair of her head; and she kissed His feet and anointed *them* with the fragrant oil. **39** Now when the Pharisee who had invited Him saw *this,* he spoke to himself, saying, 'This Man, if He were a prophet, would know who and what manner of woman *this is* who is touching Him, for she is a sinner.' **40** And Jesus answered and said to him, 'Simon, I have something to say to you.' So he said, 'Teacher, say it.' **41** 'There was a certain creditor who had two debtors. One owed five hundred denarii, and the other fifty. **42** And when they had nothing with which to repay, he freely forgave them both. Tell Me, therefore, which of them will love him more?' **43** Simon answered and said, 'I suppose the *one* whom he forgave more.' And He said to him, 'You have rightly judged.' **44** Then He turned to the woman and said to Simon, "Do you see this woman? I entered your house; you gave Me no water for My feet, but she has washed My feet with her tears and wiped *them* with the hair of her head. **45** You gave Me no kiss, but this woman has not ceased to kiss My feet since the time I came in. **46** You did not anoint My head with oil, but this woman has anointed My feet with fragrant oil. **47** Therefore I say to you, her sins, which *are* many, are forgiven, for she loved much. But to whom little is forgiven, *the same* loves little.' **48** Then He said to her, 'Your sins are forgiven.'"

To set the scene, Jesus is visiting Simon the Pharisee's home when a woman beholds upon Jesus a great act of worship, and Simon judges the woman because she came to Jesus, being in the "sinner-state" that she was in. Jesus rebuked Simon because he's been judgmental of the woman who is showing Jesus better hospitality in Simon's home than *he* is. But do you see the problem here? The only reason why Simon isn't showing hospitality is that he isn't as in tune with his spiritual need for Jesus in the same way the woman is. More directly, he's too stuck in himself and his prestige by works that he can't be in tune with his need for a Savior. Simon, *surely*, can't be in tune with his need in a way that causes him even to notice his whack hospitality, that Jesus is the Messiah, and is the One who can forgive sins. *The woman does. And you know?* Our posture should mirror the woman's attitude--so in tune with our need for Jesus by remaining in the knowledge that our nature, in its sinful state, is weak. We must **not** put **any** confidence in our flesh because of this very reason (Philippians 3:4 NKJV) that it keeps us depending on Him with a broken spirit and a contrite heart.

Luke 5:17-26 NKJV says:

> "**17** Now it happened on a certain day, as He was teaching, that there were Pharisees and teachers of the law sitting by, who had come out of every town of Galilee, Judea, and Jerusalem. **And the power of the Lord was *present* to heal them. 18** Then behold, men brought on a bed a man who was paralyzed, whom they sought to bring in and lay before Him. **19** And

when they could not find how they might bring him in, because of the crowd, they went up on the housetop and let him down with *his* bed through the tiling into the midst before Jesus. **20** When He saw their faith, He said to him, 'Man, your sins are forgiven you.' **21** And the scribes and the Pharisees began to reason, saying, 'Who is this who speaks blasphemies? Who can forgive sins but God alone?' **22** But when Jesus perceived their thoughts, He answered and said to them, 'Why are you reasoning in your hearts? **23** Which is easier, to say, Your sins are forgiven you, or to say, Rise up and walk? **24** But that you may know that the Son of Man has power on earth to forgive sins'—He said to the man who was paralyzed, 'I say to you, arise, take up your bed, and go to your house.' **25** Immediately he rose up before them, took up what he had been lying on, and departed to his own house, glorifying God. **26** And they were all amazed, and they glorified God and were filled with fear, saying, 'We have seen strange things today!'"

Here, Jesus is teaching, and the power of the Lord is present to heal the Pharisees, teachers of the law and everyone who was surrounding Him when men brought a paralyzed man down to Jesus from the housetop (they were determined…that's another story for another day). Now, the Pharisees and teachers of the law have a huge problem when Jesus forgives the sins of the paralytic, and you know why I think so? I think they wished and deemed themselves more prestigious than Jesus and believed that they should be the ones who should be given the authority to forgive sins and, "…not some carpenter." These verses signify the point I am aiming to make at this moment but will say, Friend, **works alone** do not deem or gain one anointing to walk in the power of God; the Lord deems one to walk in the power of God. Jesus is the only One who can forgive sins; the Pharisees and teachers of the law learned that on that day, even though it rubbed them the wrong way and they most likely had a problem with it because they thought they were the prestigious ones who should be forgiving sins.

The same thing could happen to us today. If we are so focused on how perfect we are or how perfect we get things correct-we won't truly realize our need for Jesus because we would be more in tune with our works rather than our needs. What will eventually happen is that our obsession with our works will not only stop us from seeing our need for Jesus, but it will also come between us fully receiving the beauty of His sacrifice. We could be saved but not have fully received what it is that He's done for us because we are more focused on our works *for* Him or our works to be approved *by* Him, *whether than focusing our affections on Him alone.* Another thing is that when we are walking in the Pharisee mindset, we want to take credit for the Lord's goodness and mercy in our lives because we are so busy looking at what we can do right that we confuse His goodness with the "accuracy" our works—*the two are not cohesive.*

This moment is not the time where you should feel shameful, embarrassed, or guilty if this is how you identify today because I understand. I understand because this was once me. Intensely insecure to the point that I allowed "my righteousness" or what I deemed to be my good works to justify me. Therefore, when I did something right, I ignorantly accounted it to how "perfect" or "good" I was or allow it to give me a sense of peace and satisfaction that should be coming from Christ and Christ alone (and I may be being a bit harsher, and matter of fact here). *This also wasn't the case.* I wasn't perfect; *I was broken.* I wasn't perfect; *I was insecure.* I wasn't perfect; *I hadn't truly understood the freedom that comes with salvation in Christ Jesus.* Not freedom to do whatever I wanted, but free to not depend on myself. *Because I simply couldn't depend on myself.*

In the same way that I deemed myself to have it all together when I got it right, I considered myself not to have it together and judged myself harshly when I got it wrong. It was a constant pull of dissatisfaction (rather I wanted to acknowledge it or not) until one day, the Lord woke me up, opened my eyes, and slowly allowed me to see the spiritual bondage and self-turmoil that I was in. This spiritual bondage kept me depending on myself to be right with the Lord; it kept me depending on myself to be pleasing before Him. And guess what? Even though I didn't know it, it kept me from fully accepting His love for me because I wasn't fully realizing and in tune with my need for Him; this cycle kept me insecure, kept me broken, and it kept me in bondage. *It kept me from seeing that I couldn't get everything right, every time, and that, that was okay.* Not getting everything right is the beauty of the Gospel; that Jesus did for you and me what we couldn't do for ourselves, which was to save our souls. *And you know what else?* He **continues** to do what we cannot do for ourselves, which is to keep our souls.

So back to that warm day in October, the Lord had spoken to me, and I realized that this was the deepest hindrance to one loving themselves the way God intended. I realized that this had once been me. And the weight of realizing that my need to get everything right was setting me up to not receive His love the way He intended me to, had me crying out to Him as I sat in this revelation.

Because you see, Beloved-Friends, fully accepting His love for me would have helped me to fully receive Him in my life and receive Him in my need, and in my dependence on Him, that I may be set free! Set free from what you may ask? **From myself! From dependence on ME!** I am not worthy to depend on myself in the way that one would depend on their Savior *because I was never meant to save myself. I was never meant to fulfill myself in and of myself, and I never could.* I am not the Savior, and I am not the Perfect One; therefore, I cannot depend on myself because I will fail myself every time.

Isaiah 2:22 NKJV says, "Sever yourselves from such a man, whose breath *is* in his nostrils; for of what account is he?" You all, I do not have it within myself to depend on myself to satisfy me—mainly to satisfy myself in Christ, and *neither do you.* Only He can satisfy us **in Him.** How could we satisfy ourselves in Him? Are we Him? *No.* So we cannot do so; we must instead, surrender and depend on Him to satisfy us in Him; **we** must rely on Him to fulfill ourselves in Him. We must look to Him to love ourselves in Him. Looking to Him is the only way that it works, Friend. There is no other way. How do we love ourselves? We genuinely accept His love for us (allowing Him to free us from our works mindset) that we may in return love ourselves through His lenses—the way He's always intended us to, which brings about so much more freedom than the counterpart.

We mustn't look to ourselves to love ourselves. We will love ourselves when we think we are worthy of it and hate ourselves when we don't. The love we need can only be gained and sustained by Someone so much greater than us—it **had** to be Jesus. So that when we do get it wrong, we rest in His Grace, and when we get it right—we account it to His goodness, His faithfulness, and His Grace. Let it be Jesus for you today. He is your source of loving yourself; *you cannot do it alone.* Love in and of yourself cannot sustain you but will fail you every time you're not satisfied, and every time you get it wrong. Your love for yourself must flow from His love for you, and you'll only find that in seeing your need for Him that you may receive His love (as 1 John 4:9 talks about it) from a place of dependence on **Him** and not *you.*

CHAPTER 7

৪৩

Love Your Neighbor

"For the commandments, 'You shall not commit adultery,' 'You shall not murder,' 'You shall not steal,' 'You shall not bear false witness,' 'You shall not covet,' and if *there is* any other commandment, are *all* summed up in the saying, namely, 'You shall love your neighbor as yourself.' Love does no harm to a neighbor; therefore love is the fulfillment of the law." ~Romans 13:9-10 NKJV

Next on the list when pursuing a lifestyle of Grace over perfection, *loving your neighbor*. After we have received the love that Christ has for us, committed to loving Him back, and then loving ourselves (*through His lenses*) we are now positioned to love our neighbors as ourselves. Essentially, what this means is that we will love our neighbors from a place of wholeness, *seeing Christ and ourselves from a proper, healthy, and Biblical lens and not from a place of dysfunction.*

During my research, I found that the commandment "(...)Thou shalt love thy neighbor as thyself" is mandated eight times in the King James Version (KJV) translation of the Bible. It's found in Leviticus 19:18, "18 Thou shalt not avenge, nor bear any grudge against the children of thy people, but **thou shalt love thy neighbour as thyself**: I am the Lord."

- Matthew 19:19, "**19** Honour thy father and thy mother: and, Thou shalt love thy neighbour as thyself."

- Matthew 22:39, "**39** And the second is like unto it, **Thou shalt love thy neighbour as thyself.**"

- Mark 12:31, "**31** And the second is like, namely this, **Thou shalt love thy neighbour as thyself.** There is none other commandment greater than these."

- Luke 10:27, "**27** And he answering said, Thou shalt love the Lord thy God with all thy heart, and with all thy soul, and with all thy strength, and with all thy mind; **and thy neighbour as thyself.**"

- Romans 13:9, "**9** For this, Thou shalt not commit adultery, Thou shalt not kill, Thou shalt not steal, Thou shalt not bear false witness, Thou shalt not covet; and if there be any other commandment, it is briefly comprehended in this saying, namely, **Thou shalt love thy neighbour as thyself.**"

- Galatians 5:14, "**14** For all the law is fulfilled in one word, even in this; **Thou shalt love thy neighbour as thyself**."

- James 2:8, "**8** If ye fulfil the royal law according to the scripture, **Thou shalt love thy neighbour as thyself**, ye do well:"

I believe that you get the point.

For something that is mentioned more than one time, even mentioned by God, Himself, through Jesus--it is worth paying attention to and consider: **what does it mean to love your neighbor as yourself,** *considering one being made whole in Jesus?*

Remember, in chapter four, when I shared my experience with the therapist? Well...I didn't quite tell you the reason why I found myself in a counseling session that day. *Here's why:*

In June of 2019, one of my closest friends and I had a disagreement. The reason why holds to many different factors that were going on that day. For example, she was helping to lead a youth service at our church and was experiencing high stress due to the heightened responsibility, preparation, and demand of the service. And me? Well, I was positioned by God to embark on one of the most difficult journeys I'd embarked on in 2019--*what it means to love your neighbor (as yourself) from a place of wholeness, despite their actions.*

You see, that day, my friend said something to me that, if I could be frank with you, rubbed me the wrong way; and it was more so of *how* she said it rather than **what** she said *exactly*. The reason why I had such a problem with it, bluntly written, is because there were some dealings from my past that the Lord had yet to address in my own heart. So in the heat of the moment, when she said what she said, *how she said it*, instead of me being understanding (whether she was right or wrong, justified or not), *I was offended.* I was more concerned with myself, rather than her. At that moment, I esteemed myself better than her, rather than in lowliness of mind, esteeming her better than myself (Philippians 2:3 NKJV). Rather than submitting to humility, I surrendered to the prideful spirit of, "*Who does she think she's talking to? I don't **ever** talk to her like that.*"

Now don't get me wrong. I am not saying that we should put ourselves, emotions, and how we receive things from other people to the side for the sake of caring for others in a way that neglects ourselves. **However**, what I am focusing on and am saying at *this* moment is that when we are whole, we respond differently to people's actions and choice of words to us--whether they are right or **not**. Understanding what I'm writing? The Lord needed to show me this...*That, that* particular day it wasn't about what she said, or even how she said it. It was about my response to it and how my response pointed to the healing that **my** heart still required.

The Word says in Luke 17:1 NKJV that it is impossible for offenses **not** to come; however, I believe the way we react to those offenses points to what's in our hearts because out of the heart flows the issues of life (Proverbs 4:23). It was vital for me to see that day that the Lord sought to work on me because if I'd focused more on my friend's actions to me, I would have missed what the Lord wanted to do in *my* heart.

From that moment, the Lord embarked me on a journey of reaching a level of wholeness that would help me to respond in love when I could be offended or even when offended; and to respond in love when I could be angry or *even when I was angry.* He taught me the foundation of what it means to be forgiving and not bitter, what it means to love instead of being resentful. What it means to seek to respect and serve, rather than seeking to **be** respected and served (no matter how I may feel about the other person's actions), and what it means to love in humility instead of walking in pride. The Lord also led me to the level of **transparency** and **vulnerability** that comes with pursuing these virtues. Like **humility** and not pride, **forgiving**, not bitterness, **love** instead of resentment, **acceptance, and forgiveness** instead of unforgiveness, and **seeking to respect and serve** rather than seeking to **be** respected and served.

Here's the thing: the reason we are offended is not that we want to be cruel at our core. The reason why we are unforgiving isn't that we like being unforgiving towards others for the fun of it or even carrying the extra mental baggage unforgiveness requires, but *it's because we are genuinely hurt; in pain.* Our response is to shield ourselves from the hurt and pain that we feel is being inflicted on us from the other individual. Hence, rather than working through the offense with the Lord, it's much easier to be unforgiving, bitter, resentful, and proud. Friends, to love our neighbor from a whole and healthy posture calls for us to have to deal with the offenses of our hearts, souls, and minds. **That**, Beloved-Friend, takes vulnerability and transparency; because when you want to shield yourself, Love--*Jesus* calls you deeper.

He calls you to enter deeper into a situation that your brain and biology has communicated to you is toxic, threatening, vulnerable, and yes, even hurtful. *Of course, this isn't in every situation.* In some situations, we **need** to flee, but in everyday offenses, this isn't the same case. In these ordinary, daily offenses, the Lord calls us to allow Him to work in our hearts what needs to be accomplished, pruned, and refined. I believe that we forfeit some relationships too prematurely because we got offended, and the relationship, and the offense and everything else simply got too hard to bear. When the truth is, the relationship confronted something within us that we weren't ready, prepared, or positioned to deal with, handle, or heal through--we weren't ready to have to deal with the pain. I believe that this is the hard truth that some of us need to hear today. *Running away from offenses and choosing bitterness, resentment, pride, and any other work of the flesh is running away from our healing and, ultimately, deeper intimacy that the Lord wants to give us in Him. We find these virtues in the places where we may be hurt or in pain the most.*

1 John 4:20 and 21 NKJV says, "**20** If someone says, 'I love God,' and hates his brother, **he is a liar**; for he who does not love his brother whom he has seen, how can he love God whom he has not seen? **21** And this commandment we have from Him: **that he who loves God *must* love his brother also.**"

Do we think people hate their brother just for the mere sake of doing so? No, some offense, and thus hurt, is usually involved. As I mentioned already but more put: when we love even amid hurt, it's us being vulnerable and transparent because we are then exposing our hurt to the source that our biology has perceived to be the root of where the injury has come from. See what I mean?

So, I had to learn what it meant to press in even while I'm hurt. I had to learn what it genuinely means to put aside pride. Because where I wanted to say, "Lord, you want me to press in? She hurt me!" I had to say, "Nevertheless, even though I'm hurt, the Lord is working on me, and I need to enter into the hurt to experience healing." In the first place, the reason why I allowed the offense to take root (not the reason why I was offended but the fact that I allowed it to birth unforgiveness, resentment, bitterness, and pride) was the **true** problem. It wasn't the offense itself *because, as I mentioned earlier, offenses will come (Luke 17:1 NKJV)*; however, it was the fact that I allowed the offense to produce works of the flesh such as pride and bitterness, for example. The fact that I allowed pride and bitterness to take over proved that somewhere deep within, there was still some healing that needed to be done. Though I had been through an extensive journey of healing, there was more restoration that needed to take place. There was some more refining that the Lord had desired in me. Plus, I simply needed to learn what it meant to love even while hurt, offended, rubbed the wrong way, etc.. The Lord hadn't been done with my healing in 2019, *just yet.*

Don't let me tell you the story and make you think that this was a quick process; **no, it was not**. It took a lot of surrendering, humbling myself before the Lord, giving up the desires of my pain and hurt of wanting to abandon my friendship with my friend, and even rationalizing why it seemed sufficient to do so. But that's the thing--that wasn't what it was all about. It was not about why I felt justified in cutting my friend off or why I "had a right" to abandon everything that we had invested in our friendship or even why it was OK to "choose what was best for me and let go of toxicity." It wasn't about any of that. Yep, you read me correctly? *It wasn't about any of that.* I had to learn what it meant to bear through confrontation even when I thought I had every reason not to--what it meant to make allowances for my friend to mess up and not expect perfection from her because **surely** I'm not perfect. I had to learn **all** of this, and this was what it was all about; this is what the Lord desired me to learn. Bearing and not giving up when things get difficult or hard. Therefore, if I would have forfeited my relationship with my friend because of her tone with me, then I would have been forfeiting the lesson Jesus wanted me to learn throughout the situation. As I alluded to before, the truth is: *it was never about the offense but what the Lord wanted to do in me.*

Anyway, this process took, on average, 5-7 months to walk through, but when I did, I experienced true and complete wholeness in the Lord (not that I'm perfect, but I am made whole by Him in this area). I learned how to let go of offenses more quickly and check pride, bitterness, and unforgiveness at the door. Furthermore, I learned how to allow the Lord to work on me when I'm hurt and offended, **without** taking it out on the other person, withholding my love and affection, exiting out of the relationship, or not loving them in the way the Lord called me to. Even while the Lord and I were working through what was in my heart. *That's right.* The Lord had to teach me what it meant to work through hurt, pain, and offense while remaining vulnerable and transparent with the other individual enough to continue the relationship with them (as best I could). The Lord was gracious enough to allow me to work through this while He worked behind the scenes to mend, fix, and heal the relationship.

I feel led to share this with you. Concerning a relationship that is God-ordained, as individuals are submitted to Him, the Lord will work out the kinks when you don't know how to; all He needs and requires is your surrendering to His will and not your will or even the will of your offense, hurt, and pain. Because you better believe, as the Lord is calling you deeper, offense (aka your flesh) will call you to chunk up your deuces and be out, aka leave the situation and the individual you perceive to have caused the pain and offense. *However, we mustn't allow that to happen; we must not allow the flesh to have its way, especially when God is calling us deeper.*

That's the place of wholeness that the Lord wants us to love our brother from. Where we say no to our flesh's way of handling offense; when we don't allow the works of the flesh involved in offenses (pride, bitterness, unforgiveness, resentment) to take root in our hearts and affect the way we love, care for, and treat our brothers. Instead, we do what Paul instructed the church of Colossi to do in Colossians 3:12-15 NKJV. It reads, "**12** Therefore, as *the* elect of God, holy and beloved, **put on tender mercies, kindness, humility, meekness, longsuffering; 13 bearing with one another, and forgiving one another, if anyone has a complaint against another; even as Christ forgave you, so you also *must do*. 14** But above all these things **put on love**, which is the bond of perfection. **15** And let the peace of God rule in your hearts, to which also you were called in one body; and be thankful." We pursue what Paul instructed while also not expecting perfection from others because perfection is only found in Jesus, Himself, the rest of us are merely striving for it, says one of the Evangelist at my church. *I truly believe and resonate with this.*

We are instead to **put on (this shows that it won't always be a natural response)** tender mercies, kindness, humility, meekness, and longsuffering while bearing and forgiving one another. In the NLT verse 13 says, "*Make allowance for each other's faults,* and forgive anyone who offends you. Remember, the Lord forgave you, so you must forgive others." We know we are walking in wholeness in our relationship with Jesus [pursuing a lifestyle of Grace over perfection with Him] when we make allowances for others' faults (*even when they're dead wrong*). Choosing forgiveness and putting on love (nevertheless), even when we are hurt, disappointed, feel let down, betrayed, and everything else this flesh is liable to experience. And to be honest, this takes a level of maturity as well, but maturity is found in wholeness; *the two co-exist together.* You can't be whole without maturity, and maturity won't be produced without a level of wholeness. I share this with you from experience. There are some things that we have to go through if we desire wholeness and maturity in Jesus; *running can't always be the answer.* We run the race with patience that is set before us (Hebrews 12:1 KJV), and a part of that is going through some things and not choosing the easier, more wide pathway of running *from* them.

1 Corinthians 13:4-8 NKJV says "**4** Love suffers long *and* is kind; love does not envy; love does not parade itself, is not puffed up; **5** does not behave rudely, does not seek its own, is not provoked, thinks no evil; **6** does not rejoice in iniquity, but rejoices in the truth; **7** bears all things, believes all things, hopes all things, endures all things. **8** Love never fails…" We know we are whole in Christ when we aim (not necessarily perfectly do) to love in a 1 Corinthians 13 kind of way despite our pain. Meaning we put our flesh under subjection to be patient and kind--bearing one another when we are working through the hurt and pain that we've experienced.

Not being bitter, upset, or reverting to dysfunctional ways of working through pain by withdrawing ourselves, lashing out, fighting, cursing, etc.. Don't get me wrong. I'm not saying this comes easy. It **is** truly a process. Having to confront hurt **is** a process; working through offenses with someone and even with Jesus **is a process.** And, you know what? Some of our journeys are different, quicker, or even slower than others, but don't allow that to be the reason why you don't engage with **your** journey, your brothers and sisters involved in your journey, and the things that Christ is trying to heal **you** from, and in return, gift you in Him.

When pursuing a lifestyle of Grace over perfection with Jesus, we only truly understand the weight of freedom when we receive healing and wholeness from past hurt and pain. *However, it doesn't stop there.* We know the influence of freedom when we use it to create a sense of hope for our brothers and sisters. *You wonder how doing so is possible?* We do this by loving them amidst their flaws/things we don't agree with that they may do, and amidst our being hurt by them; *realizing that Jesus did and continues to do this for us.* This truth, my Friend, is how pursuing a lifestyle of Grace over perfection in our relationships with Jesus can help us **genuinely** love our neighbor as ourselves—*from wholeness.* Realizing that we can, freely, love others because Jesus first loved us and the love we receive from Him is the same love in which we love one another.

I pray that this chapter only provokes you deeper into studying what it truly looks like to love your neighbor as yourself as a whole individual in Christ.

The Conclusion of the Matter:

In conclusion, the Lord's Grace is sufficient for you. His Grace, wrapped in His love, is complex enough to cover you in whatever situation you find yourself in today. Ephesians 3:17-20 NKJV says, "...that Christ may dwell in your hearts through faith; that you, **being rooted and grounded in love**, may be able to comprehend with all the saints what is the **width** and **length** and **depth** and **height-to know the love of Christ which passes knowledge; that you may be filled with all the fullness of God.** Now to Him who is able to do exceedingly abundantly above all that we ask or think, according to the power that works in us..." This is my prayer for you. Mainly that you would allow the love of God that surpasses knowledge, understanding, and any situation you can find yourself in--even in the face of the works of the flesh, to rest in your hearts. May the love of God keep you coming **boldly** to the throne of Grace, that you may obtain mercy and find Grace to help in the time of need (Hebrews 4:16 NKJV). May you know that you're worthy to depend on the Lord's Grace, even when in the face of the works of the flesh. *Man.* May you rely on Him and not yourself; may you continually find your salvation in the hands of the

Just One and not in your deeds. May you realize your deeds alone can't save you from yourself, sin, nor even the works of the flesh. Only Jesus can do that, you know? I pray you'd abide in the freedom that makes you comfortable with depending on Him and Him alone. He's waiting for you...He wants you to obtain mercy at His throne. Will you obtain the Grace your soul craves for today?

Before I go, I want to share this with you. When saved, born of the water and the Spirit (John 3:5, 8 KJV), understand that your walk with God here on earth is a journey, a pilgrimage that will lead to your eternal destination; *my prayer for you is that it'd be with Him.* To get on with my point, throughout your walk with Him on the earth, the Lord will beautify you for an eternity spent with Him. Think about it like this: your time here on earth is preparing you for an eternal *date* with your soon to come King. That's special, right? In the natural, when you think of a bride and groom, the bride beautifies herself to prepare for her wedding to the groom. She doesn't come to the wedding looking like she just rolled out of bed. No. The bride prepares herself for her union with her groom; *this is the day she's been anticipating.*

Well, because we can't prepare ourselves for the Lord's coming by our works alone, He takes the initiative of beautifying us. Isn't this beautiful? The Lord, in His sovereignty, takes the initiative to beautify us in ways that we could never do for ourselves; *He beautifies us for **His** coming— what a Gentleman!* Beloved-Friend, we were not created to clean up the mess of our sin, to carry the weight of our fleshly nature--let Jesus do that. My charge to you is to surrender to the work He's doing in **your** life. His way *(or burden)* is so much easier and lighter to carry. With this understanding is how I want you to see pursuing Grace over perfection, accepting and knowing that you can't beautify yourself for Him, so you choose to allow Him to do so--walking in full, and complete dependence on Him. Life is but a vapor (James 4:14 KJV); don't get caught up in the distractions of the enemy through the course of your time here on earth. In the wider scheme of things, it will merely be a small fraction compared to eternity with Him and not worth you stressing over. Stay on your post and allow the Lord to come in and be your Savior. Let Him carry the weight, let Him have His way. Surrender, receive Him, and patiently wait for Him to finish His work in you. He will.

My prayer for you, and I leave you with this, is that you'd believe that the glory of the Lord's Grace (Ephesians 1:6 KJV) is able to keep you, it is able to save you, and it is able to see you through. Rest in the finished work of Christ-relying on Him--knowing **HE** can keep you from falling (Jude 1:24 NKJV).

> *"Therefore we also, since we are surrounded by so great a cloud of witnesses, let us lay aside every weight, and the sin which so easily ensnares us, and let us run with endurance the race that is set before us, 2 looking unto Jesus, the author and finisher of our faith, who for the joy that was set before Him endured the cross, despising*

the shame, and has sat down at the right hand of the throne of God." ~ Hebrews 12:1-2 NKJV

With love, Your Sister,

LaGerrica

Made in the USA
Middletown, DE
15 September 2020